MANAGING STUDENT
BEHAVIOR PROBLEMS

Managing Student Behavior Problems

Daniel Linden Duke
with
Adrienne Maravich Meckel
School of Education.
Stanford University

Teachers College, Columbia University
New York and London   1980

Library of Congress Cataloging in Publication Data

Duke, Daniel Linden.
 Managing student behavior problems.

 Bibliography: p.
 Includes index.
 1. School discipline. I. Meckel, Adrienne Maravich,
joint author. II. Title.
LB3012.D84   371.5   80-10443
ISBN 0-8077-2583-8

Designed by: Julie E. Scott
    7 6 5 4 3 2 1
  86 85 84 83 82 81 80
Manufactured in the U.S.A.

This book is dedicated to Joshua, whose only discipline problem is his father, and to Sergei Rachmaninoff, who should be held accountable for stirring Slavic souls. In addition, it is dedicated to the students in the Spring 1979 edition of Education 347 at Stanford and to Dorothy Brink.

Contents

Preface

THIS BOOK SPEAKS TO the individual who feels that schools are not dealing with student behavior problems as effectively as they could. In calling for changes in the handling of "school discipline," we do not mean to imply, however, that educators have necessarily been careless or inept. We believe that the vast majority of those engaged in schooling are doing the best they can — under circumstances that would wither a martyr's faith! The public expects today's schools to respond to a growing list of needs that other sectors of society are no longer willing or able to satisfy, at the same time that greater accountability is being demanded and financial support of schools is being curtailed.

The audience to whom we address the following chapters includes teachers, school administrators and other school personnel, policymakers, parents, teacher educators, and, in some instances, students. We have tried to minimize the amount of technical language and concepts in the book, though periodically we shall need to refer to organizational theory or to review the results of research studies related to school discipline. Most of the book is as applicable to elementary as to secondary schools, to private as to public schools, and to non-American as well as American schools.

Our approach in this broad appeal is *organizational*. To the extent that all schools share certain common organizational characteristics (i.e., rules, decisions, rewards, sanctions, communications), we can talk in terms applicable to a wide range of educational settings.

We attempt to accomplish three objectives in this book. First, we discuss the alternative control procedures available to educators faced with student behavior problems. Next, we build a case for one particular set of control procedures — those related to problem management — and finally tell how to implement them. The book is divided into three sections, each encompassing one of these objectives.

Our recommendations are derived from a variety of sources, including practitioners' reports of effective techniques, research studies, evaluations of schools, organization theory, and — not least — our own experiences as educators. We do not intend the recommendations solely for the fabled inner-city high school besieged by severe and frequent student behavior problems. Our ideas should also be of benefit to those in less tense situations who are committed to enhancing their school's credibility as a rule-governed organization.

A final word of clarification: though we use terms like "discipline" and "management," we do *not* intend the ideas discussed herein to constitute a call for more "back to basics" regimentation or for less concern with student rights. Neither do we count ourselves members of that amorphous group of educators who decry all constraints on student conduct. In other words, we do not regard school discipline as a zero-sum game — in which either students or school personnel must lose. Rather, our plea is for more thoughtful, careful and well-coordinated management of procedures by which schools can respond effectively to student behavior problems.

D.L.D.
A.M.M.

PART I

Overview: Alternative Control Procedures

1

Confronting Student Behavior
Problems—
What Are the Alternatives?

O UR PURPOSE IN THIS chapter is to identify alternative responses available to school personnel faced with student behavior
problems. Once we have presented and discussed these alternatives, we shall look at how educators in three real schools—an elementary, a junior high, and a senior high school—respond to one
particularly troublesome behavior problem—illegal absenteeism.

THE CASE FOR CONTROL

All organizations confront behavior problems on a daily basis.
Sometimes the behaviors belong to employees, sometimes to clients.
To the extent that these behavior problems interfere with the ongoing operation of the organization, they may require a formal response. According to various theorists, mechanisms for controlling
the behavior of an organization's members are necessary to prevent
disorder (entropy) and facilitate the efficient achievement of the
organization's foals.[1] Etzioni defines organizational control structure as "a distribution of means used by an organization to elicit the
performances it needs and to check whether the quantities and qual-
ities of such performances are in accord with organizational specifi-
cations.[2]

Schools confront control problems that are more complex and
perplexing in some ways than the problems faced by many other organizations, such as commercial businesses and factories. The control structure of the school must contend not only with employee
behavior, but with client (student) behavior as well. If recent reports are accurate, problems involving student behavior have

3

reached alarming numbers, particularly at the secondary level.[3] These reports indicate that student behavior problems — ranging from truancy and disrespect for authority to violence and vandalism — are interfering with the ability of educators to accomplish their objectives.

A wide assortment of student behavior problems have been identified. They can be placed into five major categories:

I. Attendance-related problems
    A. Absence from school without permission (truancy)
    B. Absence from class without permission (skipping, cutting)
    C. Late arrival to school or class (tardiness)
    D. Leaving school without permission

II. Out-of-class problems
    A. Criminal behavior
        1. Physical assault and battery
        2. Extortion; intimidation
        3. Theft
        4. Possession of weapons
        5. Possession, use, or sale of controlled substances
        6. Destruction of property (vandalism)
        7. Bomb threats
        8. Setting false fire alarms
    B. Noncriminal behavior
        1. Fighting (without injury)
        2. Cigarette smoking (outside of designated smoking areas, where they exist)
        3. Use of "nuisance" equipment on school property (radios, skateboards, etc.)
        4. Littering
        5. Loitering in halls or unsupervised areas
        6. Public displays of affection
        7. Improper attire
        8. Disruptive behavior on school bus or at an extracurricular activity

III. In-class behavior
    A. Classroom deportment

  1. Talking or answering out-of-turn
  2. Disrespect toward the teacher
  3. Disrespect toward another student
  4. Disruptive behavior
  5. Chewing gum or eating
  6. Moving around the classroom without permission
B. Conduct related to academic work
  1. Failing to complete assignments
  2. Not completing assignments on time
  3. Forgetting equipment (pencil, textbook, etc.)
  4. Cheating on tests
  5. Copying homework from another student or plagiarism
  6. Failing to prepare for class (i.e., not suiting up for P.E. class)

To deal with student behavior problems such as those outlined above, educators commonly rely on a variety of relatively formalized approaches or techniques, hereafter referred to as *control procedures*. Control procedures are distinguishable from less formalized or deliberate control actions, such as those that might result spontaneously when a person in a position of authority is compelled to act without reflection. A control procedure implies some degree of intentionality and planning, as well as organizational legitimacy. A teacher's striking a student in self-defense when caught by surprise or setting up a spur-of-the-moment faculty vigilante committee to avenge a malicious act thus would not be regarded as organizational control procedures.

After scanning the literature on classroom management and schoolwide discipline policies, as well as works dealing with general organizational control, the authors have decided to group control procedures into clusters, based on common goals and target groups. These clusters we shall refer to as *control* strategies.

Field research we have conducted suggests that educators often fail to consider all the possible control strategies available to them before they decide on a particular course of action.[4] If failure to review alternative strategies characterizes other schools besides the ones we have investigated, it would help explain the contemporary crisis in school discipline and the seeming inability of educators to control dysfunctional behavior. The likelihood of making an effective decision is increased by expanding the number of alternatives that are considered.[5] We hope that the following attempt to identify alternative control procedures and strategies will assist educators concerned with improving disciplinary decision-making and researchers interested in studying this process.

CONTROL STRATEGIES

Table 1 lists six general control strategies available to educators faced with student behavior problems. We believe that these strategies encompass most, if not all, of the possible options. The fact that each strategy is discussed separately in the following pages does not imply that several different strategies cannot be in effect simultaneously or that particular strategies do not overlap each other in certain respects. Conceivably in some schools *no* control strategy may be operative.

As mentioned earlier, each strategy can be characterized in at least two ways — by its goal and by its target group. Goals range from the avoidance of problems to problem management. Target-groups cover a similarly wide range of choices, from the students accused of problematic behavior to the victims of such conduct. A strategy not only may accomplish an intended goal; it also may produce unintended by-products, both negative and positive. The ensuing discussion will look at the goals, target-groups, and possible by-products of the six strategies.

Problem Avoidance

Problem avoidance may occur because a teacher is unaware that certain problematic behavior is taking place. This phenomenon, well-described by Kounin as a lack of "withitness," is not, however, the kind of problem avoidance we address in this paper.[6] To think that a strategy can be based on a lack of awareness we consider a contradiction in terms. Strategies, by their very nature, imply cognizance and intentionality.

Table 1
Control Strategies for Dealing with Behavior Problems

Name/Goal of Strategy	Target	Specific Control Procedures
Problem avoidance	Persons accused of problem behavior	Selective ignoring
Problem acceptance	Rule-makers Rule-enforcers	Elimination of rules
Problem compensation	Victims of behavior problems	Restitution, sympathy, protection
Problem prevention	Persons likely to cause behavior problems in the future or those who come into contact with them	Rules, sanctions, rewards, curriculum adaptation, curriculum augmentation, self-esteem enhancement, parent education
Problem intervention	Persons accused of problem behavior	Directive communication, nondirective communication, behavior modification, sanctions, problem referral, parental involvement
Problem management	Situations that tend to produce problems	Special personnel, team troubleshooting, data collection, conflict-resolution procedures, decentralized authority, smaller organizational units, environmental redesign

On occasion, a teacher actually may be aware of problematic behavior, but lack the time, skill, or resources to deal with it. Under these circumstances cognizance exists, but no strategy is selected.

For present purposes, we will represent problem avoidance as a deliberate decision not to deal with problematic behavior, because of a belief that avoidance will result in elimination of the problem or prevention of a worse problem. Perhaps the most frequent use of this strategy is made by advocates of behavior modification, who often urge educators to overlook mildly disruptive conduct, thereby denying to students the potential reinforcement of their attention. Sometimes teachers also may intentionally opt to avoid dealing with a problem because they fear intervention could lead to a more serious one. The feared consequences of intervention can range from student verbal abuse to physical attack. Teachers in one study, in fact, report that they do not patrol areas known to be sites of illegal student activities.[7] Apparently, the teachers feel that a single teacher should not jeopardize his or her safety doing "police" work. A third instance when problem avoidance may be used is when teachers wish to spare themselves the potential embarrassment of making an effort to establish order and then failing to do so in front of a group of students. Thus, teachers pretend on occasion not to hear a derisive student comment or not to see an aggressive act.

Little research has been done on the impact of problem avoidance when it is elected out of fear or in order to save face. We find it difficult to imagine, though, that widespread problems such as extortion, intimidation, and drug selling — so often traced to poorly supervised parts of the school such as stairwells and bathrooms — will decrease because adults avoid supervising student "turf".

Problem avoidance as systematically practiced by behavior modifiers *has* been studied; and the evidence suggests that ignoring certain problem behaviors, when coupled with the reinforcement of appropriate behavior, can reduce classroom problems among elementary-age students.[8] We caution teachers adopting an "ignoring" strategy, though, to expect an escalation of behavior problems before a drop finally occurs.

Despite the reported success of problem avoidance by behavior modifiers, several concerns arise. Ignoring negative behavior presumes that the purpose of the behavior is for the student to obtain teacher or class attention. If a student possesses a different reason for being disruptive (i.e., seeking revenge), ignoring the behavior may have undesirable consequences. A second possible problem relates to the issue of generalizability. Since few studies have looked at problem avoidance with adolescents, it is unclear whether the strategy is effective in high schools, where most behavior problems seem to occur. Adopting problem avoidance in a high school setting may unduly endanger other students.

Problem avoidance probably is appropriate for certain kinds of problems and not others. Mildly disruptive conduct, particularly where intended as an attention-seeking device, thus may disappear if teachers simply overlook its occurrence. The question remains, though, whether teachers and other students can tolerate the situation while waiting for the problem behavior to abate. Behavior modifiers sometimes neglect the impact of problem avoidance on teacher morale and class climate, or else they study the strategy in experimental settings where competing demands of teachers and students have been controlled. Advocates of problem avoidance need to specify with greater clarity the circumstances under which use of the strategy can be most effective in reducing student behavior problems without deleterious side effects for teachers.

Problem Acceptance

The term "problem acceptance" may be slightly misleading. We shall use it to describe situations in which behavior that once was regarded as unacceptable is reconsidered and labeled acceptable. The repeal of Prohibition and the decriminalization of marijuana possession in some states are notable examples of problem acceptance. In some ways schools have moved more slowly than other sectors of society toward accepting previously unacceptable behaviors. While new rules are continually added to school codes of conduct, rarely are old rules reconsidered or eliminated.

Alternative schools may be exceptions to the preceding statement. A study of California alternative high schools indicates that most of them function quite effectively with a minimum number of proscribed behaviors.[9] Some alternatives specify only one or two rules, usually concerning attendance and respect for the rights of others. Behaviors such as smoking, profanity, and occasional tardiness generally are allowed, though not encouraged. The fact that the alternative schools in the study did not report serious behavior problems is particularly impressive considering that they typically enroll large percentages of students previously identified as "behavior problems".

Deciding to adopt a problem-acceptance strategy entails answering three basic questions, two dealing with ethics and the other with practicality.

The two ethical questions go as follows: Is it right for schools to classify as unacceptable for students certain behaviors deemed acceptable for adults? And is it fair for schools to promulgate rules restricting the behavior of all students when evidence exists that only a small minority are guilty of causing problems?

The first question queries the legitimacy of double standards. Examples of double standards in schools are numerous. Students often are forbidden to smoke cigarettes while teachers are not. Students must turn in assignments on time, but teachers may take weeks to return corrected papers. The arguments usually heard to support the double standards include the belief that students are not mature enough to behave responsibly and the notion that the maintenance of order and the protection of students preclude too much student freedom. Both arguments have flaws. Most students do, in fact, act responsibly most of the time. In addition, many school rules exist less for the welfare of students than for the convenience of educators.[10]

The second ethical question is foreshadowed by the first. If a minority of students is responsible for most of the behavior problems in schools, why should everyone be restricted? Philosophically, it may be preferable to handle behavior problems on an individual basis rather than to implement general rules; but practically speaking, individualizing discipline is not easy. To some extent, schools are bureaucratic organizations, and teachers function as civil servants. As a result, all students are expected to receive equal treatment. Can a teacher, for example, punish a student who constantly interrupts for talking out-of-turn, while ignoring the same conduct when it is exhibited by another student who rarely talks in class?

The third question involves a different aspect of problem acceptance. How capable are schools of enforcing rules restricting student behavior? Our assumption underlying this pragmatic query is that making rules that cannot be enforced reasonably well is undesirable.[11] Perhaps educators should cut down on the number of rules simply in order to increase their ability to enforce effectively the rules that remain. Such a suggestion promises to enhance the credibility of the school as a rule-governed organization and to reduce teacher frustration related to rule enforcement.

Critics of problem acceptance may claim that it represents a capitulation to wrongdoers and does nothing to reduce the incidence of problematic behavior. Little is known of the effectiveness of the strategy in actually lessening the frequency or severity of behaviors previously prohibited. The repeal of Prohibition did not eliminate alcoholism, of course; but neither did Prohibition. Permitting pregnant girls to attend regular classes — and therefore removing pregnancy from the list of "discipline problems" — succeeded in permitting teenage mothers-to-be to continue their formal education and therefore restored to them a basic constitutional right; but it is hard to determine whether or not this course of action, by appearing to constitute official approval of teenage pregnancy, actually contributed to an increase of births by adolescent mothers.

Problem Compensation

As a strategy, problem compensation can supplement other strategies or stand alone. Since it emphasizes assisting victims rather than confronting the perpetrators of problems, this strategy, when it does stand alone, seems to constitute tacit recognition that one cannot confront the behavior problem in question directly with much success. A recent example of problem compensation has been the action by several states to create insurance coverage for victims of certain crimes. Persons attacked or robbed by unknown assailants thus may ask the state to help cover damages. Another example is the establishment of special shelters for battered wives and abused children.

Schools have not provided much in the way of problem compensation, despite indications of increasing student and teacher victimization.[12] Thus, a visitor to school who slips on a wet floor and breaks a pair of glasses may be covered by the school's liability insurance; but a student whose coat is stolen from a locker has little recourse.

One reason why schools may have been slow to adopt problem-compensation strategies, particularly where students are involved, is the prevailing belief that victims "asked for it" or contributed in some way to their own victimization. As William Ryan suggests, this policy of "blaming the victim" may characterize much of society, not just the schools.[13]

To speculate on possible negative by-products of problem compensation it is conceivable that where such strategies are not accompanied by efforts to combat the problematic behavior itself, they serve to syphon off resources that otherwise may be committed to problem prevention, intervention, or management. Also, a program to assist victims can contribute to a sense of complacency among officials, thus undermining attempts to mobilize support for efforts to attack behavior problems directly. As long as victims are being cared for, there may not be a sense of urgency concerning the implementation of other strategies.

The first three strategies — problem avoidance, problem acceptance, and problem compensation — are not classical *control* strategies per se. One might argue, in fact, that they constitute the antithesis of control strategies — desperate measures occasioned by a perceived inability to deal directly with problem behavior. We include these strategies in the present scheme, however, because they do constitute alternative courses of action for school personnel to consider. Each has the potential to preserve some semblance of organizational stability, if not complete control, thereby facilitating efforts by members to achieve organizational objectives.

The next three strategies — problem prevention, problem intervention, and problem management — represent more clearly recognizable control strategies. Unlike the previous three, each of which is relatively undifferentiated, the following strategies subsume a variety of different control procedures.

Problem Prevention

For several decades, prevention has been almost as sacred a concept as progress once was to progressives. To be taken seriously, social welfare programs have been compelled to include prevention components that seek to ferret out the "root causes" of problems and eliminate them. The belief that prevailed until recently has been that complex social problems could be solved if enough money and outside expertise were brought to bear. Schrag characterizes this thinking, so reminiscent of the Kennedy-Johnson era, as "the impossible dream."[14] Several decades of impossible dreams have suggested, however, that prevention is easier sought than accomplished. Recent governmental moves, as characterized by the formation of the National Institute for Education's "Local Capacity for Problem Solving" Group, represent more modest and localized efforts to deal with school problems.

We find it necessary to describe the dimensions of prevention strategies in relation to the last two strategies — problem intervention and problem management — because the three often overlap in the minds of educators and can easily be confused. Sometimes, for instance, prevention is given such a broad definition that it seems to encompass both intervention and management. For the purposes of the present analysis, though, we feel that the three should be clearly delineated.

As Table 1 indicated, prevention strategies primarily concern those individuals judged likely to become behavior problems in the future. Intervention strategies, as the name implies, involve actual, rather than potential problems. Hence, emphasis is placed on dealing with individuals already manifesting (or accused of manifesting) problematic behavior. The primary objective of intervention strategies is the *elimination* of existing behavior problems rather than the prevention of problems anticipated to occur in the future.

Problem management strategies focus on *problematic situations*, rather than on particular individuals. Generally these strategies seek to reduce behavior problems indirectly by changing organizational factors instead of people. Unlike the previous two strategies, problem management is based on the belief that behavior problems cannot be totally eliminated or prevented from recurring. Rather than vainly striving for these goals, emphasis is placed on moderating or "managing" the impact of problematic behavior so that it does not become dangerous or disrupt the pursuit of organizational objectives. Problem management will serve as the focus for our succeeding chapters.

Notes

1. Amitai Etzioni, "Organizational Control Structure" in James G. March (ed.), *Handbook of Organizations* (Chicago: Rand McNally & Company, 1965); Arnold S. Tannenbaum, "Control in Organizations" in Arnold S. Tannenbaum (ed.), *Control in Organizations* (New York: McGraw-Hill Book Company, 1968).

2. Etzioni, p. 650.

3. George H. Gallup, "Tenth Annual Gallup Poll of the Public's Attitude Toward the Public Schools," *Phi Delta Kappan,* 60, 1 (September 1978); National Institute of Education, *Violent Schools-Safe Schools,* Vol. I (Washington, D. C.: U. S. Department of Health, Education and Welfare, 1978); Robert Rubel, *The Unruly School* (Lexington, Mass.: Lexington Books, 1977); Edward Wynne, "Adolescent Alienation and Youth Policy," *Teachers College Record,* 78, 1 (September 1976): 23-40.

4. The authors appreciate the support of the National Teacher Corps in their efforts to study how educators respond to student behavior problems.

5. Irving L. Janis and Leon Mann, *Decision Making* (New York: The Free Press, 1977); Herbert Simon, *Administrative Behavior* (New York: The Free Press, 1976).

6. Jacob S. Kounin, *Discipline and Group Management in Classrooms* (New York: Holt, Rinehart and Winston, Inc., 1970).

7. Daniel L. Duke, "Adults Can be Discipline Problems Too!" *Psychology in the Schools,* 15, 4 (October 1978): 522-528.

8. W. C. Becker, *et al.,* "The Contingent Use of Teacher Attention and Praise in Reducing Classroom Behavior Problems," *The Journal of Special Education,* 1, 3 (Spring 1967): 287-307.

9. Daniel L. Duke and Cheryl Perry, "Can Alternative Schools Succeed

Where Benjamin Spock, Spiro Agnew, and B. F. Skinner Have Failed?" *Adolescence,* 13, 51 (Fall 1978): 375-392.

10. Daniel L. Duke, "Looking at the School as a Rule-Governed Organization," *Journal of Research and Development in Education,* 11, 4 (Summer 1978): 116-126.

11. *Ibid.*

12. National Institute of Education, *Violent Schools-Safe Schools* (Washington, D.C.: U.S. Government Printing Office, 1978).

13. William Ryan, *Blaming the Victim* (New York: Pantheon Books, 1971).

14. Peter Schrag, "End of the Impossible Dream," *Saturday Review* (September 19, 1970): 68-69.

2

Using Problem Prevention, Intervention, and Management

HAVING BRIEFLY CHARACTERIZED THE last three strategies at the close of Chapter 1, we now wish to discuss problem prevention in greater detail. It is important to recall that prevention, like intervention, focuses on individuals or groups rather than organizational factors. This tendency to overlook the influence of organizational factors on the behavior of members of the organization constitutes a major concern with these two approaches. There are other concerns as well.

PROBLEM PREVENTION

One of the hardest tasks involved in problem prevention is to identify individuals likely to manifest behavior problems. The science of predicting human behavior is still in its infancy. Efforts to identify behavior problems can backfire into self-fulfilling prophecies.

Prevention obviously depends on the capacity to isolate so-called "root causes" of problematic behavior. Exploring the etiology of behavior problems can be quite complex, since multiple variables typically are involved. School personnel may not possess the time, resources, or expertise required for the task. In addition, many of the causes of school behavior problems presumably lie outside of school. So far, collaborative ventures involving schools and other social agencies have not proved very successful on a long-term basis.

Despite these concerns, a variety of prevention strategies have been proposed and attempted in recent years. A list of some of the better-known approaches together with the causal factors to which they presumably respond follows:

Prevention Strategy: Control Procedures	*Causal Factors Addressed by Procedure*
1. Rules	Lack of defined behavioral limits.
2. Sanctions	Lack of sufficient "costs" for inappropriate behavior.
3. Rewards	Lack of reinforcement for appropriate behavior.
4. Curriculum adaptation	Irrelevant learning outcomes. Curriculum unsuited to student ability level.
5. Curriculum augmentation	Failure on the part of students to acquire prerequisite skills, knowledge, and/or attitudes necessary for appropriate behavior in school.
6. Self-esteem enhancement	Lack of feeling of accomplishment by students. Cycle of failure.
7. Parent education	Lack of good parenting at home. Conflicting norms between school and home.

The first two examples have tended to exemplify administrative practice in the past. The standard response to increased student behavior problems traditionally has been more *rules* and/or harsher *sanctions*. Although the student rights movement and several recent court cases have challenged a variety of school rules (i.e., dress codes) and sanctions (i.e., suspension), we find little evidence that actual school practice has changed much.

The use of formal rules is based on the somewhat cynical belief that students will tend to misbehave unless external limits are placed on their behavior. Such a belief derives some legitimacy from religious notions of "original sin" — in other words, from the viewpoint that in the absence of established authority, humans (particularly immature humans) will act selfishly and irresponsibly.

A corollary of this belief is that rules are more useful when promulgated before being needed rather than afterwards.

The prior existence of sanctions, along with rules, long has been regarded as a deterrent to problem behavior. Recent public manifestations of this thinking are demands for the reinstatement of capital punishment, public flogging, and other forms of corporal punishment. Some of the sanctions currently used in schools to deal with rule-breakers include spanking, paddling, detention, withdrawl of privileges, lowered grades, and suspension.

Despite the popularity of rules and sanctions, the evidence concerning their effectiveness is mixed. The previously cited study by Duke and Perry suggests, in fact, that the absence of long lists of rules and harsh sanctions may help produce better student behavior. Too many rules, for example, may actually contribute to the creation of behavior problems by overtaxing the capacity of teachers and administrators to enforce them, thereby leading to inconsistent discipline, teacher frustration, and the undermining of the school's credibility as a rule-governed organization. Hargreaves, Hester, and Mellor, reporting on one of the most extensive studies of school rules to date, conclude that "in some schools some of the rules could be abolished without any serious consequences." They go on to say,

If a rule is not strictly necessary or does not serve any really important purpose, might not its abolition — and the abolition of all its associated deviance — be in the best interests of all? . . . teachers might devote greater attention to examining the pupils' perspective on rules, for they may not always understand or share the teachers' justification for rules. Research has shown . . . that where teachers enforce rules which are seen by some pupils as illegitimate, the enforcement of the rules may provoke an entirely unintended and unanticipated widespread deviance.[1]

Sanctions, as well as rules, present certain problems. For example, some sanctions, such as suspensions, may serve more as rewards than as punishments for certain students who dislike school. Dreikurs argues that many traditional punishments lack any logical relationship to the offense for which they are intended.[2] He advocates replacing strictly punitive sanctions with "logical consequences." Behavior modifiers criticize sanctions from a different angle, claiming that they are less effective than the reinforcement of appropriate behavior. Unfortunately, using systematic reinforcement seems to be more difficult for many educators than simply threatening to use sanctions. When reinforcement is used, it tends to be employed as an intervention rather than a prevention procedure. Thus, a student who is a chronic behavior problem may be offered a reward if he or she exhibits improved conduct. Such use of reinforcement as an intervention procedure can backfire, of course, if students who generally are well-behaved begin to wonder why they do not receive any rewards or if students misbehave purely in order to receive reinforcement.

In two general ways the curriculum can be enlisted to prevent behavior problems. *Curriculum-adaptation procedures* are based on the belief that the curriculum in some ways contributes to the onset of behavior problems, either by appearing irrelevant to students or by failing to correspond to student ability levels (i.e., too challenging or not challenging enough). Specific curriculum-adaptation procedures include elective courses of special interest to students, career-education programs and work study opportunities, and courses designed to accommodate students at several ability levels. While not a curriculum procedure per se, early graduation is yet another possible component of a prevention strategy, one particularly appropriate for students who have completed all of their regular curriculum requirements and who are growing restless waiting to graduate.

Curriculum-augmentation procedures derive from the fact that course content can serve as a *cure for,* as well as a *cause of,* behavior problems. An underlying assumption of these strategies is that particular students misbehave because they simply have not learned how to behave properly or because they lack the values that would result in acceptable conduct in school. Among the curriculum-augmentation procedures identified by Duke are the following: deportment training, moral education, values clarification, and effective education.[3] The little research that exists on these approaches fails to demonstrate their general effectiveness as prevention procedures, though they may work well for particular students.

Self-esteem enhancement as a prevention procedure is based on the well-documented fact that many students, particularly those from disadvantaged backgrounds, do not feel capable of succeeding in school. The result often can be failure, followed by frustration and eventually by behavior problems. To prevent the commencement of this "failure cycle", some educators advocate providing high-risk students with opportunities for which success can be guaranteed. Support for such self-esteem enhancement programs comes from the work of Glasser.[4] Whether insulating students from failure is preferable to teaching them that failure can be instructive, however, is still a debatable question.

Many educators, when faced with chronic student behavior problems, tend to attribute them, at least in part, to "problems at home." Accusations range from too much parental discipline to too little, to lack of consistent discipline. Single parents are popular targets for blame. *Parent-education programs,* as another control procedure aimed at prevention, thus are designed to inform parents of the ways their behavior can influence the behavior of their children. Again, we note a lack of research on the efffectiveness of these programs; but many teachers believe that the parents who participate in such programs are not the ones who need them.

Assessing the impact of school prevention strategies presents a variety of problems. First, what criterion is to be used to determine if a behavior problem actually has been prevented? Total elimination? Significant reduction? For what length of time must a problem have been in remission to enable a strategy to be judged effective?

Second, to what extent are prevention programs legal and/or ethical? We have already mentioned the possibility of self-fulfilling prophecy. Can schools justify special programs for students identified as "potential" behavior problems? In light of the absence of foolproof predictors of those students, what is the school's legal liability in cases of erroneous prediction?

This second problem suggests a third one. In the attempt to prevent misbehavior, schools actually may cause other problems. For instance, parent-education programs may alienate community members who feel they are being scapegoated for the school's failure to handle its own problems. Curriculum augmentation may result in charges that the school is trying to teach values. Minorities are particularly sensitive to this kind of issue. The use of certain rules (dress code) and sanctions (suspensions) can result in action restricting the prerogatives of educators to control students.

In addition to these specific backfire-effects, prevention strategies may occasion more general concerns. Does the very selection of a *prevention* strategy, for instance, create the unreal expectation that longstanding and complex problems actually can be prevented? If such an impression is created and if, in reality, most problems are endemic to schools, then questions must be raised about the value of raising false hopes, which can only lead to subsequent disillusionment. Also, strategies encompassing more rules or harsher sanctions seem to punish all students for the transgressions of a relative few. Prevention strategies must be deterred from punishing students who consistently behave appropriately.

PROBLEM INTERVENTION

While some educators and a host of social scientists have urged the adoption of prevention strategies, others, many of whom are "in the trenches" daily, contend that intervention is the only realistic course of action. As indicated in the last section, intervention strategies seek to eliminate behavior problems, or prevent their recurrence, among individuals already manifesting the problematic behavior.

Critics of intervention claim that it offers only "Band Aid" solutions that do little to reduce the likelihood of future problems. Further, intervention strategies usually do not call for a deep understanding of the causes of behavior problems. Defending the use of intervention strategies, advocates stress the need to restore order quickly when problems arise. They usually cannot afford the luxury of contemplating questions of etiology and diagnosis. In this regard, Stebbins points out that "the events of the schoolroom allow little opportunity for reflection."[5] He feels it impractical to expect teachers to confront every behavior problem with the care so often required by those espousing prevention.

By talking with teachers and administrators and by reviewing the literature on classroom management, we have identified a variety of intervention procedures.[6] Among the most widely cited are the following:

Intervention Strategy: Control Procedures	Operational Examples
1. Directive communication	Embarrassment, intimidation, commands
2. Nondirective communication	"Active listening," negotiations, counseling
3. Behavior modification	Systematic reinforcement
4. Sanctions	Detention, extra assignments, loss of privileges, corporal punishment, suspension
5. Problem referral	Send student to office or resource person
6. Parental involvement	Parent-teacher conference, parent contract

Directive communication probably is the most frequently employed intervention procedure, perhaps because it is among the simplest to use. Asking a student to stop an annoying behavior, calling attention to the behavior in such a way as to embarrass the student, and issuing threats or warnings all are time-honored techniques for trying to establish classroom order. Also included in this category are certain nonverbal forms of communication, such as touching a student, moving toward a student in an authoritative manner, and using a signal, such as raising a finger to the lips or switching off the lights. Observations in classrooms suggest that directive communication can be an effective way of dealing with minor disruptions, but that it does not appear to be useful with serious disturbances. In addition, ethical questions may be asked concerning the use of some directive communication approaches, such as embarrassment.

Nondirective communication derives, in part, from the work of "humanistic" psychologists such as Carl Rogers. Its basic principle is that annoying behavior should be regarded not as a problem but as an opportunity. In other words, such behavior is simply another way by which students convey their upsets and needs. Alert teachers thus can follow up on these behavioral signals with conferences and advisement to determine what is troubling students. Teacher Effectiveness Training contains several suggestions for nondirective communication, including "active listening" and a six-step negotiation process aimed at conflict resolution.[7] DeCecco and Richards report on the success of another type of conflict resolution procedure, one particularly suited to schoolwide problems.[8] One key factor in explaining the low level of behavior problems in alternative high schools may be the ready availability of teachers to listen to troubled students and help resolve problems on the spot.[9] Often minor upsets can be prevented from growing into major disturbances merely by providing students with immediate opportunities to express what is bothering them instead of deferring intervention or sending students elsewhere. Kindsvatter concludes, "all things considered, and excluding the early childhood levels, the most effective control technique for serious misbehavior is the private teacher/student conference.[10] He goes on to note that

It has the disadvantage of being time-consuming and difficult to schedule, but it does provide an opportunity away from the stress of the classroom and the presence of the student's peers to examine the behavior in question.

A third intervention procedure is *behavior modification,* a convenient rubric under which to place an array of techniques derived from the work of behavioral psychologists. We have already mentioned systematic reinforcement of appropriate behavior as a prevention procedure. More often than not, however, behavior modification is employed as a way of dealing with *existing* behavior problems. A considerable body of research attests to the effectiveness of various kinds of reinforcement, extinction, desensitization, token economies, and other behavioral approaches.[11] An important element in the success of these techniques may be their emphasis on realistic behavioral expectations. Behavior modification protocols avoid calling for the overnight eradication of problematic behavior. Generally they suggest a more realistic, gradual reduction of such behavior to tolerable levels. This characteristic of behavior modification procedures eliminates much student and teacher frustration.

Advocates of behavior modification prefer positive reinforcement to negative reinforcement or punishment. Many educators, though, continue to rely on sanctions to obtain desired behavior. *Sanctions* are regarded as procedures of intervention as well as prevention. In the earlier discussion of sanctions, we questioned their efficacy. Assigning extra homework as a sanction, for example, may simply teach students to regard homework as punitive rather than helpful. Restricted study halls are subject to similar criticism. A second problem with many sanctions is that they affect different students in different ways. Thus, some students may consider suspension as aversive while others view it as rewarding.

Of course, to change the way sanctions are employed in schools is not a simple matter. Although a case may be made that sanctions should be individualized to fit the particular student, such a policy in reality would run the risk of public criticism. Parents may applaud individualized instruction, but many would regard individualized discipline as unfair, particularly if their children received sanctions considered to be more severe than those meted out to other children.

Problem referral is a fifth type of intervention procedure, one that sometimes can be viewed as a sanction, depending in part on the destination of the referral and its purpose. Referral can be an acknowledgment that the person reporting the behavior problem is unable or unwilling to handle it. Gordon observes that teachers rarely sit down with students to try and resolve problems together.[12] When a teacher cannot deal with a behavior problem, he or she typically refers the student to a dean or vice principal. Some maintain that a majority of such referrals inevitably come from a small fraction of the faculty. In any event, if the administrators cannot solve the problem, they may refer the student to a guidance counselor. The counselor, in turn, may send the student to a school psychologist or social worker. In this entire referral process, the idea is rarely stressed that the student should share some of the responsibility for diagnosing the problem and prescribing a solution.

Today, although more resource people are available to whom to refer troubled students, fewer individuals are willing to assume responsibility for intervention and follow-up. Most persons to whom referrals are made function primarily as consultants, offering advice and short-term contact, but avoiding continuing involvement and supervision or accountability.

Parental involvement is another intervention procedure often utilized by teachers and administrators, but one the effect of which is poorly understood. Educators complain at times that the parents of "problem" students, particularly those from lower-class neighborhoods, refuse to get involved in school-based intervention efforts. Parents, for their part sometimes are intimidated by visits to school administrators and other times resentful that they are only called by the school in times of crisis. When parents actually can become involved in the resolution of behavior problems, many educators believe that the likelihood of problem recurrence is greatly reduced.

As in the case of prevention strategies, intervention strategies may occasion certain backfire-effects that result in the continuation or intensification of the very problem they seek to moderate. For example, directive communication can provoke angry displays of behavior by students who feel the need to "save face" in front of their peers. Nondirective communication may become so satisfying to certain attention-deprived students that they "misbehave" in order to have the opportunity to meet with a caring adult. Research to date has said little to the educator about the negative by-products of intervention or the specific circumstances under which intervention strategies are most appropriate.

PROBLEM MANAGEMENT

The final type of strategy is based on the belief that behavior problems will always exist. Metz notes in her observation of schools that students invariably challenge their teachers' authority.[13] Some students probably will feel restricted no matter how few rules exist. Almost a half-century ago, Waller commented that "The fundamental problem of school discipline may be stated as the struggle of students and teachers to establish their own definitions of situations in the life of the school.[14]

If behavior problems are endemic to schools, then emphasis on prevention may be misplaced. Instead, schools need to develop an ongoing capacity for confronting problems and reducing the likelihood that they will get out of hand. Problem management presumes that certain situations tend to give rise to behavior problems (i.e., receiving a low grade, being asked to sit down and be quiet) and that certain organizational responses minimize the negative impact of these situations. By anticipating these situations and encouraging thoughtful organizational responses, school personnel may be able to "manage" many problems. In other words, the focus of problem management is how to change organizational factors rather than individuals.

Problem-management strategies are a relatively new addition to the educator's repertoire of approaches to student behavior problems. Only in the past few decades, in fact, has interest begun to shift from dealing with problems on an individual or classroom basis to a schoolwide level.[15] Among the specific problem-management procedures we cite the following:

Management Strategy:
Control Procedures   *Characteristics*

1. Special Personnel   Deans, security guards, para-
                                professionals, crisis teachers
2. Team troubleshooting   Early problem detection and
                                mobilization of resource peo-
                                ple
3. Data collection   Monitoring trends in behavior
4. Conflict-resolution
     mechanisms   Formal grievance process and
                                negotiated solutions
5. Decentralized authority   Student and teacher involve-
                                ment in decision making
6. Smaller organizational units Alternative schools, mini-
                                schools, "the house system,"
                                learning communities
7. Environmental redesign   Removal of temptations and
                                creation of pleasant sur-
                                roundings

While we will have more to say about problem-management procedures in subsequent sections of the book, it may be useful to review some of them now. One widely used problem-management procedure involves the use of *special personnel* to monitor behavior problems.[16] Among the relevant role groups now found in many schools are deans of students, teacher aides, security officers, school social workers, crisis teachers, community liaisons, and attendance clerks.

To date, the impact of special personnel on the overall level of student behavior has not been widely studied. A New York school official reports that his system's single most effective management strategy is "the use of trained security personnel, capable of responding to emergencies and sufficiently mobile to move through the building under the direction of experienced supervisors."[17] But greater numbers of special personnel may not always mean fewer problems. Perhaps the presence of more people dealing exclusively with behavior problems will result in the identification of many previously undetected problems. In some cases, individuals actually may provoke new behavior problems by inviting challenges to school authority! Experience with demonstrations in the 1960s has led many police departments to employ lower "profiles" and more plainclothes personnel in certain situations so as to defuse climates conducive to confrontation.

Special personnel may provide valuable input for a second problem-management procedure — *team troubleshooting*. This procedure involves the pooling of perceptions of teachers and other persons concerned with particular groups of students (i.e., all ninth graders) in order to facilitate the detection of incipient problems. Later in this book, we will outline several guidelines for effective troubleshooting sessions. For example, troubleshooting should lead to specific courses of action for specific students, and each strategy should have one person responsible for seeing that the strategy is tried and assessed. Should a course of action fail to ameliorate the situation, what may be needed is more focused troubleshooting, perhaps entailing a case conference. Case conferences permit the involvement of special resource people, such as school psychologists, youth workers, relatives, or friends of the troubled student. A survey of secondary schools in New York and California indicates that many principals employ some form of troubleshooting, but it is unclear how effective these efforts are.[18]

Team troubleshooting is related to a third problem-management strategy — *data collection.* The availability of accurate, up-to-date data on the nature and extent of student behavior problems is important for the development of effective strategies. Data permit school personnel to concentrate on priority problems, anticipate future concerns, combat rumors and set realistic objectives involving the improvement of student behavior. If, for example, one knows that most of the. disciplinary referrals are coming from a small group of teachers, the organizational response may be quite different than it would be if most of the faculty are sending students to the office. Despite the value of accurate data on student behavior problems, many administrators have difficulty maintaining systematic records beyond student attendance and suspension statistics. Faced with growing crime problems, schools in large cities are being compelled, however, to ensure that incidents are recorded better. For instance, Philadelphia schools must maintain special "incident reporting desks" where behavior problems can be catalogued and analyzed.

A fourth management procedure — *conflict-resolution mechanisms* — overlaps the nondirective communication category of problem-intervention strategies. Techniques such as those described in the previous section not only can function as immediate outlets for student upsets and teacher frustrations; they also can function as effective managerial devices for encouraging students and school personnel to deal with areas of disagreement in a constructive fashion. In addressing the need to "routinize" conflicts in schools, Corwin makes the point that:

Schools need a procedure to handle organization-based grievances — that is, problems that go beyond the individual's interests and personal problems. For, whereas people are normally inclined to defend their own interests . . . they need additional protection and incentive to raise questions about . . . the system itself.[19]

A fifth procedure — *decentralized authority* — is consistent with the spirit underlying the preceding one. Both suggest that more responsiblity for dealing with problems of student behavior should be assumed by the principal parties involved — students and teachers. Research by McPartland and McDill indicates that behavior problems tend to be less frequent in schools where students feel more involved in decision-making.[20] Findings from the study of alternative schools by Duke and Perry support this idea.

Many administrators appear reluctant to permit much decentralization of their authority in matters related to school discipline.[21] If ways of overcoming administrators' concerns can be found, students and teachers might participate in a variety of activities including the determination of rules and the consequences for disobeying them, the enforcement of rules, and the designation of school objectives concerning student behavior.

One way to facilitate decentralization is to subdivide large schools into *smaller organizational units* — a sixth problem-management procedure. Evidence of the popularity of this approach can be found in the proliferation of alternative schools, Individually Guided Education (IGE) learning communities, and house systems. Dividing schools into smaller units promises to reduce student alienation and increase the opportunities available for meaningful interaction between students and teachers.

A final, related example of a management procedure is *environmental redesign*. An assumption underlying this approach is that a drab, barren, uninspiring learning environment helps create situations where behavior problems are more likely to occur. A second rationale for environmental redesign is somewhat at odds with the preceding one. In the latter instance, the reason for changing the environment is to eliminate tempting targets for vandalism and areas that cannot be easily supervised by school personnel. Ways to achieve this objective include graffiti-proof wall coverings, removal of "useless" windows, burglar-proof doors, and minimally exposed bathroom fixtures. The question that remains for creative architects and interior designers is whether or not school environments can be both pleasant to live in and vandal-resistant.

As in the case of the other five types of strategy, problem management has the potential to backfire. Mention already has been made of the possibility that special personnel may actually encourage student challenges to authority. Other possible negative by-products include teacher resentment over requests to keep accurate data on student behavior problems and to join with students in making disciplinary decisions. Subdividing schools may lead to more homogeneous grouping and the elimination of relatively low-use, high-cost instructional opportunities, such as foreign-language laboratories and vocational courses.

Notes

1. D. H. Hargreaves, S. K. Hester, and F. J. Mellor, *Deviance in Classrooms* (London: Routledge & Kegan Paul, 1975), p. 256.

2. Rudolf Dreikurs and Loren Gray, *A New Approach to Discipline: Logical Consequences* (New York: Hawthorn Books, Inc., 1968).

3. Daniel L. Duke, "Can the Curriculum Contribute to Resolving the Educator's Discipline Dilemma?" *Action in Teacher Education*, 1, 2 (Fall-Winter 1978); 17-36.

4. William Glasser, *Schools without Failure* (New York: Harper & Row, Publishers, 1969).

5. R. A. Stebbins, "The Meaning of Disorderly Behavior: Teacher Definitions of a Classroom Situation," *Sociology of Education*, 44, 2 (Spring 1970): 217-236.

6. Daniel L. Duke (ed.), *Classroom Management*, The Seventy-Eighth Yearbook of the National Society for the Study of Education, Part II (Chicago: The University of Chicago Press, 1979).

7. Thomas Gordon, *T.E.T.: Teacher Effectiveness Training* (New York: Peter H. Wyden, Publisher, 1974).

8. John P. DeCecco and Arlene K. Richards, *Growing Pains* (New York: Aberdeen Press, 1974).

9. Daniel L. Duke and Cheryl Perry, "Can Alternative Schools Succeed where Benjamin Spock, Spiro Agnew, and B. F. Skinner Have Failed?"

10. R. Kindsvatter, "A New View of the Dynamics of Discipline," *Phi Delta Kappan*, 59, 5 (January 1978): 322-325.

11. Harvey F. Clarizio, *Toward Positive Classroom Discipline* (New

York: John Wiley & Sons, Inc., 1976); Howard N. Sloane, *Classroom Management* (New York: John Wiley & Sons, Inc., 1976); Carl E. Thoresen (ed.), *Behavior Modification in Education,* The Seventy-second Yearbook of the National Society for the Study of Education (Chicago: The University of Chicago Press, 1973).

12. Thomas Gordon, *T. E. T.: Teacher Effectiveness Training.*

13. M.H. Metz, "Clashes in the Classroom: The Importance of Norms for Authority" (A paper presented at the annual meeting of the American Educational Research Association, March 1978).

14. Willard Waller, *The Sociology of Teaching* (New York: John Wiley & Sons, Inc., 1932), p. 297.

15. Daniel L. Duke, "A Systematic Management Plan for School Discipline," *NASSP Bulletin,* 61,415 (January 1977): 1-10

16. Daniel L. Duke, "How Administrators View the Crisis in School Discipline," *Phi Delta Kappan,* 59, 5 (January 1978): 325-330.

17. National School Public Relations Association, *Violence and Vandalism* (Arlington, VA: NSPRA, 1975), p. 22.

18. Daniel L. Duke, "How Administrators View the Crisis in School Discipline."

19. Ronald G. Corwin, *Militant Professionalism* (New York: Appleton-Century Crofts, 1970), p. 355.

20. James M. McPartland and Edward L. McDill, *The Unique Role of Schools in the Causes of Youthful Crime,* Report No. 216 (Baltimore: Center for Social Organization of Schools, 1976).

21. Daniel L. Duke, "How Administrators View the Crisis in School Discipline."

3

Learning from Field Observations

A RESEARCH STUDY IN WHICH the authors have been engaged has focused on disciplinary decision-making and organizational control structures in three urban California schools that constitute a "feeder system" — a senior high school, a junior high school that serves the high school, and an elementary school that serves the junior high. By conducting field observations in these schools, attending meetings, interviewing school personnel on a regular basis, and reviewing disciplinary documents, we have been able to determine which control procedures are in effect and to estimate their effectiveness. While a full report of these data will appear elsewhere, we would like to highlight here some of the findings to illustrate points made in the previous chapters and pave the way to recommendations in upcoming chapters.

The major student behavior problems at all three schools are related to attendance — truancy, tardiness, and cutting class. Teachers complain that the students who most need to be in class typically are those who are late or absent. To sustain academic growth in classes where sometimes as many as half the students are missing is a task that teachers perceive to be virtually impossible. On many occasions, students come to the junior and senior high schools, but fail to attend any classes. Instead, they socialize with their friends and try to avoid getting caught. When students are illegally absent from class, school personnel suspect that they often are engaged in dangerous or illegal activities.

VARIED RESPONSES

The response to attendance problems varies somewhat among the three schools. Each school uses different procedures for different types of truant students; coordination of control structures among the three schools is virtually nonexistent. The control of student-attendance behavior is highly idiosyncratic, varying within each school as well as among them. Control structure seems to depend, to some extent, on the time of the year, the age of the students, the size of the school, the nature of school leadership, and a variety of other factors.

At the high school, which enrolls about 1400 students, problem-acceptance strategy characterizes the administration's approach to many chronic truants. Thus, despite the State's requirement that all students under the age of eighteen receive instruction, school personnel acknowledge that students who manifest little desire to attend school are, in effect, allowed to drop out. Administrators claim they would need additional resources to seek out these students and lure them back to school. Such resources are unavailable at present, in part because of the loss of local revenues occasioned by declining enrollments and a taxpayers' revolt.

Students who are judged to have the potential to complete high school occasionally are lured back, but only when someone on the staff is willing to assume personal responsibility for tracking them down and providing ongoing support. School personnel agree that the key to effective intervention is personal commitment. Unfortunately, few formal rewards are available to encourage teachers and other school personnel to make such commitments.

Where used to reduce attendance problems, rewards tend to be employed to gain the compliance of chronic truants. Students who consistently attend school, however, receive no such rewards. One particularly attractive reward offered to some truants is placement in the school's alternative program — a less-formal school appendage designed to accommodate approximately 100 students who seem incapable of abiding by conventional behavioral expectations. The program has few official rules. Not surprisingly, more students want to participate than can presently be accommodated; but plans exist to expand the program. The daily attendance rate is about 95 percent, higher than for the regular high school.

Another component of the high school control structure involves problem management. Through quarterly reports, parents are kept informed about the attendance of their children. Many persons view this procedure as ineffective, however; they suspect that students intercept the reports before they reach parents. Even if the computerized forms do reach parents, such reports are difficult to interpret. In addition, nine weeks is felt to be too long a period of time between notification attempts. Efforts to make daily phone calls to parents of absent students were tried with some success, but budget cuts forced the abandonment of this project.

When illegal student absences appear to be increasing, the standard response of the high school administration is to 1) invoke new sanctions or make existing sanctions more harsh and 2) step up enforcement efforts. Suspensions are still used to punish some truants, despite the fact that such sanctions often are viewed by students as rewards. Detention after school has begun to be used, however, as a more logical sanction. The ability of the school administration to maintain detention facilities depends on the willingness of teachers to share the task of monitoring the operation. In reaction to threatened staff-cuts, teachers have refused to undertake such monitorial duties, thus undermining any administrative effort to initiate a "crackdown" on illegal absences.

Ironically, the refusal of teachers to serve as detention monitors has not stopped the "crackdowns." Off-duty police and campus supervisors (paraprofessionals) have been employed to report students caught loitering in the halls who should be in class. Thus, the number of students being referred to detention hall for illegal absences continues to increase, despite the fact that the facility cannot accommodate additional students. Like planes circling a busy airport, students wait for weeks before "working off" their detention time. This situation illustrates the need for greater within-school coordination of control procedures.

In addition to employing problem-acceptance, problem-intervention, and problem-management strategies, the high school until recently attempted some problem prevention as well. Counselors received extra pay in the summer to visit the homes of all incoming ninth graders and to inform students and parents of attendance rules as well as other behavioral expectations. Unfortunately this program had to be eliminated because of budget cuts.

The picture one gets of the high school control structure as related to one set of problems — illegal student absences — is incredibly complex and somewhat dismaying. A variety of procedures representing different control strategies are or have been in effect, but they do not seem to have been arrived at through systematic decision-making or evaluated carefully. The role groups that are most affected by the control procedures — the students who are subject to the procedures and the teachers who often must implement them — have not participated on a regular basis in the review or adoption of procedures. Most people, when questioned about the control structure regarding student absences, complain that no uniform or generally accepted approach exists. Rules concerning attendance are perceived to be enforced inconsistently. In addition, sanctions for those who do not attend school seem to be applied inconsistently as well. Coordination of different procedures often is lacking — a fact that sometimes results in one control procedure's undermining another.

Many of the above observations also pertain to the junior high school, but certain differences in control structure do exist. The junior high no longer possesses an alternative program for students with attendance problems. The program, which operated on a makeshift basis for several years, had to be axed because of staff cuts. A second difference is related to the age of junior high students. Junior high school officials are not as free to employ a problem-acceptance strategy as their high school counterparts. Thus it is less easy to permit chronic truants to drop out of school.

None of the three schools possesses effective parent-notification procedures, standardized techniques for maintaining up-to-date records on student absences, or the troubleshooting mechanisms necessary for early intervention with students. The elementary school, however, has begun to develop a systematic problem-management strategy encompassing a variety of procedures, including daily phoning of parents whose children miss school, standard forms for reporting student absences, and teacher teams that meet to try and anticipate student problems before they get out of hand. Plans have been formulated to involve parents, students, and teachers in developing a uniform set of school and classroom rules and sanctions. An orientation film, to be created by teachers and students, will be shown to all new students in an effort to alert them to behavioral expectations at the school.

In summary, the three schools have utilized a variety of procedures representing almost all of the six general control strategies in an effort to ensure that students attend school and conduct themselves appropriately while in attendance. The fact that absenteeism and other student behavior problems have not disappeared, and in some cases actually have increased, thus deserves careful consideration. Possibly the continuation of the problems is related less to a procedure itself than to the way it has been adopted and implemented.

ORIGINS OF THE SCHOOL'S RESPONSES

Unfortunately, we have had great difficulty in tracing the origins of many of the control procedures currently in use in the three schools under investigation. In talking with school personnel in the junior and senior high schools, however, it becomes clear that disciplinary decisions often are made on an informal basis, without systematic evaluations of previous control procedures and policies, thorough searches for alternative procedures, brainstorming, careful speculation on possible consequences of particular procedures, or concerted efforts to involve key role groups — including parents, counselors, teacher aides, district resource persons, and students. No teacher interviewed in either the junior or senior high school recalls any meeting being held that was devoted specifically to making decisions concerning absenteeism or other student behavior problems. While we cannot conclude that the apparent absence of formalized disciplinary decision-making contributes directly to the continuation or increase of student behavior problems, we find it hard to imagine that the haphazard assortment of control procedures that have arisen out of the informal and unsystematic interactions of a few administrative personnel has helped school discipline in any significant way.

We realize that our observations are based on field studies in just three schools, but our previous experience coupled with reports from educators suggest that the problems we have identified can be found in other schools as well. While trying to explain why the selection and coordination of control strategies may tend to be informal and unsystematic is beyond the scope of this chapter, we believe it may be useful to speculate briefly on several possible reasons.

Systematic decision-making of the kind advocated by organization theorists requires considerable time and motivation. Both of these resources are currently lacking in our two secondary schools (and we suspect in other schools as well). However tempting it may be to grow impatient with the way educators often go about determining school control structure, prudence calls for remembering the scarcity of these resources and the reasons they are scarce before launching into yet another attack on schools.

School personnel are barraged by a steady flow of problems. Budget cuts, as indicated earlier, have reduced the total number of school personnel, thus placing greater pressure on those who remain. Effective programs have had to be eliminated or scaled down. Extra time for assessing current control procedures, reviewing alternatives, and undertaking careful deliberation prior to making disciplinary decisions simply does not exist. Time taken for such activity often is time taken away from other, more valued endeavors such as instruction. Careful planning and systematic decision-making can be expected in the long-run to contribute to a reduction in student behavior problems, but in the short-run these processes actually may add to existing problems by overextending school personnel.

Even if school personnel were willing to think in terms of the eventual payoff of disciplinary planning and decision-making, it is not at all clear that most would be sufficiently motivated to engage in these processes. Educators are demoralized by demands for better education amidst public efforts to reduce educational appropriations. Many teachers, even those with considerable experience, are uncertain whether their jobs will be available from one year to the next. Job insecurity hardly is conducive to long-range planning.

DIFFERENCES AMONG THE SCHOOLS

Having cited reasons why some schools may be characterized by unsystematic disciplinary decision-making, we nonetheless must note that the elementary school in the present study has been able to undertake the development of a logical, coherent set of control procedures. What characteristics of the elementary school help to explain why it has not suffered the same organizational problems as the junior and senior high schools?

One of the most obvious differences is size. The smaller size of the elementary school means that fewer teachers must be consulted during the process of deliberating and adopting control procedures. Coordination of procedures that are implemented is easier for the same reason. Efforts to involve parents and students in decision-making also require less time and energy.

Other differences include the nature of student behavior problems and the utilization of outside technical assistance. Student behavior problems at the elementary school, while significant, are not as extensive as or, at times, as serious as problems in the secondary schools. Elementary teachers feel that if matters grow too bad, they can always resort to their authority to gain student cooperation. This option is not always effective when employed with older students. In addition, the elementary school, largely through the initiative of its principal, is making extensive use of outside technical assistance provided by a federal grant to the district. This assistance is contributing to the development of control procedures of the problem-management variety. While the junior and senior high schools also have access to this expertise, they have been slower to take advantage of it.

THE CASE FOR PROBLEM MANAGEMENT

In the last section of this chapter we make a case for the problem-management strategy as the approach most likely to produce these needed alterations in school organization. By now it is becoming clear that we find great merit in the problem-management strategy. Our assessment derives from three basic reasons.

First, this strategy is *realistic,* in that it assumes that behavior problems can never be totally eliminated. In certain cases, such problems may even be desirable![1] Problem-management procedures seek to prevent behavior problems from getting out of hand, rather than to stop them from occurring altogether. A second desirable feature of problem-management procedures is their *humanistic* quality. Unlike some other approaches, problem management assumes that repeated student behavior problems often indicate that certain aspects of the school organizational structure are not responding as well as they could to student needs. Thus, emphasis is placed on changing school organization rather than students. Attempts to change students directly are considered only as a last resort. A final reason for preferring problem-management procedures concerns their *practicality*. Lasting improvements typically depend on changes at the managerial level. Other types of innovations — such as new instructional techniques and curriculum materials — tend to ignore the importance of administrative support in ensuring the success of new ideas.

Systematic Management Plan for School Discipline

The remaining chapters of this book cover a series of recommendations on how to reduce student behavior problems through problem management. The plan is a collection of "best existing-practices," as related by practitioners and suggested by research findings in the area of school discipline. In many ways it represents an idealized model for dealing with student behavior problems. The authors know of no single school that embodies all of the suggestions covered in the following chapters, although a number of schools currently are attempting to implement many of them.

The Systematic Management Plan for School Discipline is founded on two fundamental premises: to be effective, control procedures must be 1) applicable on a schoolwide rather than a class-by-class basis and 2) comprehensive rather than partial.

The first premise suggests that teachers who give up on their colleagues and decide to content themselves with establishing order in their own classrooms make it more difficult to establish a truly schoolwide plan for managing behavior problems. For at least four reasons, a schoolwide approach to the reduction of student behavior problems is preferable to a series of individual classroom efforts.

• First of all, the majority of serious student behavior problems —

at least the ones that perplex educators the most — do not occur in class. Instead, they take place before school, between classes, after school, on the bus, in the cafeteria, and at athletic events and dances. These are occasions when adult supervision tends to be lacking. Stressing better classroom management techniques probably does little to eliminate these out-of-class behavior problems. Only well-coordinated initiatives on a schoolwide basis can maximize the likelihood of meaningful improvements.

• Second, a major source of concern on the part of students, parents, and school administrators seems to be teacher inconsistency. One teacher enforces certain rules that another teacher ignores. Such inconsistency undermines student respect for the school as a rule-governed organization. Not very much can be done to reduce between-teacher inconsistency without members of the school community working together in a collaborative manner.

• A third reason for schoolwide discipline plans relates to contemporary legal developments. Where once educators enjoyed the broad discretionary powers of parents in dealing with their students, they now face the possibility of court review of their actions. The courts have upheld the principle that students have constitutional rights. Any abridgement or denial of these rights — as might occur in the daily administration of school discipline — may result in a lawsuit. As a result, it behooves educators to develop consistent, schoolwide disciplinary policies that acknowledge the rights of students.

• A final reason for preferring a schoolwide approach concerns the importance of administrative support in the success of any effort to improve school discipline. Various studies have noted the crucial role played by the principal in any school-improvement attempt.[2] If teachers are content to get their own classrooms in order and avoid collaborative approaches aimed at developing effective schoolwide plans, they minimize the likelihood of obtaining administrative support.

Key Organizational Components

The second major premise on which the Systematic Management Plan for School Discipline is based concerns the desirability of comprehensive — rather than piecemeal — change. Often well-intentioned efforts to innovate have foundered because attention was given to changing only one dimension of schooling. Schools, of course, are complex systems with a variety of interrelated parts. To try and alter one part, for example the curriculum, without changing other parts, such as reward structure (which provides incentives for teachers to master new content) or the evaluation system (which determines whether students are succeeding or not) is naive. Sarason contends that innovations that ignore the "existing regularities" of schools are foredoomed.[3]

The Systematic Management Plan for School Discipline is based on the belief that a school consists of interdependent organizational components, many of which exert some impact on the creation and resolution of student behavior problems. Seven key organizational components are identified in the chapters to follow. They include:

1. School rules and sanctions
2. School records and information-processing
3. Conflict-resolution procedures
4. Troubleshooting mechanisms
5. Community involvement
6. Environmental design
7. Staff development

This book contends that the probability of reducing student behavior problems will be increased by considering how well each of these organizational factors is functioning and how they relate to each other.

CLOSING THOUGHTS

The fact that the Systematic Management Plan for School Discipline concentrates on problem management should not be construed as an indictment of the other five control strategies. Each may be of some use under certain circumstances. We believe, though, that educators who feel the need to work on improving school discipline can maximize their impact by considering the following set of problem-management recommendations.

The next seven chapters discuss in detail the above key dimensions of school organization. In some schools certain recommendations already will be in effect. So much the better. Readers are urged, however, to remember the need for comprehensiveness. The concluding chapter is intended as a guide to those serious about implementing the Systematic Management Plan for School Discipline.

Since schools are subject to a variety of internal and external pressures to change, particular recommendations, from time to time, are likely to prove to be inadequate, unnecessary, unworkable, or undesirable. Any management plan, to be realistic, must be evolutionary and responsive to changing conditions. The authors invite readers who have direct experience with particular recommendations and who feel they require modification to contact us.[4] In this way we hope to assure that the Systematic Management Plan for School Discipline will continue to be timely and responsive to the needs of school personnel and students.

Notes

1. Consider, for example, the student who grows disruptive because he or she is threatened, in need of attention, or concerned about an abridgement of personal rights. The disruptive behavior actually is healthy in such cases.
2. National Institute of Education, *Violent Schools - Safe Schools* (Washington, D.C., U.S. Government Printing Office, 1978); Seymour Sarason, *The Culture of the School and the Problem of Change* (Boston: Allyn and Bacon, Inc., 1971).
3. Seymour Sarason, *The Culture of the School and the Problem of Change.*
4. Please send letters in care of Professor Daniel L. Duke, School of Education, Stanford University, Stanford, California 94305.

PART **II**

The Systematic Management Plan for School Discipline: Key Organizational Components

4

Understanding the School as a Rule-Governed Organization

RULES CONSTITUTE ONE OF the central features of school organization. They presumably exist to enable the school to achieve its objectives in a relatively efficient and fair manner. When student behavior is judged to be problematic, the judgment typically is based on the student's failure to observe a rule. School personnel expend considerable time and energy in an effort to enforce rules and handle instances of rule-breaking behavior. Rules thus afford a logical place to begin thinking about a plan for improving school discipline.

> **Goal Number 1:** Create an awareness on the part of all who work and study in the school that it is an organization governed by rules.

The rules that govern and guide behavior in schools are not always accorded the same respect that laws mandated by legislative bodies consisting of elected representatives command. Is it because the state has more power to enforce laws? Are the state's penalties for disobedience more severe? Or do school rules and regulations receive less respect because they do not derive from "the people?" Each of the factors raised in these questions probably helps to explain why rule disobedience in schools has persisted over the years.

The last factor will serve as our focus for this chapter. How can schools increase the degree to which teachers, students, and parents regard the school as a rule-governed organization?

Eleven hypotheses characterizing school rules in the United States have been proposed by Duke:

1. School rules and the consequences for disobeying them tend to be determined by those groups or individuals least subject to their application.
2. School rules and the consequences for disobeying them are not communicated effectively to students or parents.
3. Many teachers find it difficult to enforce school rules consistently.
4. The rules which students disobey most are those which either 1) relate least clearly to popular perceptions of school functions, 2) are communicated least well to students, or 3) are enforced least consistently by teachers and administrators.
5. School rules typically are regarded by teachers and administrators as ends in themselves, rather than means to more productive learning.
6. The consequences for disobeying school rules frequently lack a logical relationship to the offenses.
7. Accurate records concerning violations of school rules generally are not maintained by school authorities.
8. Students have few options if they disagree with a charge brought against them by school authorities.
9. School rules are rarely evaluated in a systematic way.
10. The school rules which are enforced most actively are those designed for the protection or convenience of teachers and administrators.
11. Teachers often fail to model good rule-governed behavior.[1]

The Systematic Management Plan for School Discipline (SMPSD) is based on the belief that schools can increase their credibility as rule-governed organizations by encouraging the collaborative development of discipline policies, rules, conflict-resolution procedures, and consequences for disobeying rules. To achieve such broad-based participation, educators must come to regard schools as communities of individuals sharing common goals and certain basic rights. Gwynn Nettler has stressed the importance of this "sense of community" in reducing crime and juvenile delinquency.[2] In a study of student behavior in public alternative schools, behavior problems were found to be minimal where students and teachers share responsibility for developing and enforcing rules.[3] A study of several urban high schools found that students who felt the most involved in school rule-making tended to report having fewer behavior problems.[4] Lawrence Kohlberg, writing on the progress of the "just community" school-within-a-school in Cambridge, Massachusetts, observed that positive changes in student behavior could be attributed directly "to the sense of community which . . . emerged from the democratic process in which angry conflicts are resolved through fairness and community decision."[5]

A SENSE OF "OWNERSHIP" IN THE SCHOOL

Creating a feeling among students that they share in the operation of schools is a key element in the encouragement of productive student behavior. Educators, however, are sometimes threatened because they feel that student involvement in rule-making will lead to student challenges to teacher authority in other areas, such as subject-matter knowledge and evaluation. Students generally realize, though, that teachers have greater expertise in these areas.

> **Recommendation Number 1.1:** *Collaborative development of school rules.* School and classroom rules as well as the consequences for disobeying them should be decided collaboratively among teachers, students, administrators, and parents.

Implementing the first recommendation is no easy matter. It is difficult to involve more than a few students in rule-making, for example, because gatherings of entire student bodies require time. Time is usually the most precious commodity in any school. In addition, many students feel uneasy about working together with teachers. Often the students sense that they are not really considered equal partners in decision-making. Interestingly, teachers often feel the same way about administrative efforts to implement shared decision-making.

The response of school officials to the issue of greater student involvement in decision-making typically has been to establish student governments with faculty advisors. In many cases, however, these groups have been unable to provide students with a real feeling of influence.[6] Students recognize, as did Seymour Sarason, that *teachers* make classroom rules.[7] In a study of student attitudes in several California high schools, investigators learned that students disliked having few opportunities for meaningful participation in decision-making.[8] In another study — this time involving urban, suburban, and rural high schools — students expressed a strong interest in helping with classroom planning, school policymaking, and discipline.[9] Eighty-one percent of the students claimed that their most violated right was teacher respect for their opinions. John DeCecco and Arlene Richards, questioning thousands of high school students in New York and California, discovered that fewer than one student in every five felt they had a voice in the resolution of problems in which they personally were involved.[10]

Several recent blue-ribbon commissions charged with making recommendations on how to improve American secondary education have urged school officials to provide opportunities for greater student involvement in school governance. Both the White House Conference on Youth and the National Panel on High School and Adolescent Education endorsed the belief that students have a right and responsibility to be involved in decisions concerning school rules, curriculum, and teacher evaluation.[11]

It is futile to search for efficient or expedient ways of regularly involving students in decision-making related to school and classroom rules. Efficiency and expediency are not necessarily desirable objectives, however, where democratic process is concerned. Decision-making takes time, patience, and reflection. Still, there doubtless are ways that school officials can facilitate student participation.

One possibility entails restructuring large schools to form several smaller "learning communities." This tactic, epitomized by mini-schools, schools-within-schools, and Individually Guided Education programs, permits greater schedule flexibility and a more community-oriented climate, both important elements in democratic decision-making. Another tactic entails using the first week of school to develop a "sense of community." Sometimes schools arrange for retreats or camping trips during this period. These occasions help students get to know one another and develop feelings of mutual trust and cooperation.

Critics of student involvement in rule-making may argue that such activities divert students and teachers from the primary function of schools — namely, the acquisition of basic skills. Few can dispute the fact that recent years have witnessed an ever-growing number of nonacademic expectations being placed on schools. Many of these expectations, including such items as drug education, nutrition information, and child-abuse monitoring, seemingly have little to do with the so-called "basics." Granted, the schools cannot achieve all of these aims without either eliminating other expectations or supplementing existing personnel. Schools are unprepared to replace families as the primary guardians of youth welfare. Despite these factors, however, it would be a serious mistake for educators to take such a narrow view of school goals that they ignore entirely matters of citizenship and social adjustment.

Emphasizing the "basics" has been interpreted to mean that schools strive to prepare students for life after they graduate. Schools, however, involve twelve years of actual living as well as preparing for "life." It is morally imperative, administratively prudent, and eminently sensible for educators to devote some portion of their time and effort to improving the quality of life *in schools*. Subject-matter knowledge and proficiency in academic skills may be of little benefit to students if they cannot coexist with others or function in a group setting. An old joke tells about an illiterate individual who was jailed for picking pockets. While in prison, he was taught to read and write. Because of his progress in learning "the basics" he was granted a parole. Soon, however, he returned to prison — but this time for forgery!

Arguments for improving the quality of life in schools are not new. For over a century critics have called for more humane schools and teachers who are interested in the "whole" student. In a recent attempt to present ideas for reforming secondary education, Task Force '74, funded by the Kettering Foundation, linked improvements in the quality of school life to the proliferation of alternative learning opportunities and to the increase of opportunities for students to exercise responsibility.[12] The SMPSD is based on the belief that student behavior will improve when school personnel begin to treat students more responsibly.

EMPHASIZING STUDENT RESPONSIBILITY

One way to encourage students to exercise responsibility is to teach them to be responsible. Responsibility, like reading, is learned through practice. Teachers may begin in the early grades by treating rules as subject matter worthy of serious study. After all, young people desiring a driver's license must pass a test on traffic rules. Why not teach students about rules and then test them on it? Including references to school rules and the consequences for disobeying them in regular classroom discussions can demonstrate to students that such matters are just as important as dangling participles and Millard Fillmore's presidency! Teachers should not assume that students understand how they are expected to behave in school. Several studies have suggested that students are uncertain about how to act.[13] A recent Gallup Poll indicated that the public wants more classtime devoted to teaching students how to behave appropriately.[14] The message is clear — school rules and issues related to student behavior belong in the regular academic curriculum.

> **Recommendation Number 1.2:** *Rules-related content incorporated in academic curriculum.* Skills, attitudes, and content related to school rules, rule-making, and the nature of rule-governed organizations should be incorporated into the regular academic curriculum of the school.

Here are some ways that student behavior and related topics can be addressed within the context of the regular academic curriculum:

1. Analyzing values and the ways individuals develop their own.

2. Teaching specific values necessary for the perpetuation of society.
3. Discussing human behavior in general and student behavior in particular.
4. Teaching group dynamics skills that can be useful in resolving conflicts related to behavior problems.
5. Teaching school rules and the consequences for disobeying them.[15]

In recent years a variety of programs have been developed to increase student awareness of themselves, their behavior, and the world in which they live. Values-clarification activities employ hypothetical situations and forced-choice techniques to stimulate students to consider why they act in certain ways. "Self-sciencing," "reality therapy," and Program TRIBES are current group-dynamics strategies that utilize actual student concerns to foster discussions about personal feelings.[16] A particularly comprehensive approach to student behavior is provided in the "Curriculum in Moral Education for Adolescents" by Ralph Mosher and Paul Sullivan.[17] This curriculum, intended for high school juniors and seniors, consists of four phases: 1) personal introductions, 2) discussion and analysis of moral dilemmas through case studies, 3) learning counseling skills, and 4) teaching high school students to be moral educators with younger children.

In many ways, the most ambitious attempt to address student behavior through the curriculum has been made by moral-development theorist Lawrence Kohlberg and social-studies expert Edwin Fenton. They have implemented their ideas in a pair of alternative schools that seek to establish a "just community." Students are taught how to function in a rule-governed organization and how to be contributing members of a democratic microsociety.[18]

Dorothy Kobak's approach differs from the one presented by Kohlberg and Fenton. Her program seeks to improve student behavior by increasing interpersonal sensitivity.[19] She has created a curriculum unit devoted to teaching emotionally disturbed and socially maladjusted children to care about each other. Kobak's work underscores the fact that educators must not assume that students, particularly those with psychological problems, know how to treat each other with respect. All students probably can benefit from training in interpersonal relations.

The most direct curricular approach to student behavior would involve actually teaching students school rules and the consequences for disobeying them. Little evidence exists, however, to indicate that such instruction is available in public schools. A study we completed on discipline in New York and California high schools, for example, found that students are rarely tested on rules.[20] Teaching students school rules and then testing them would eliminate the possibility that students could claim they were unaware of a rule when they disobeyed it.

One reason why school rules rarely become subject matter is that teachers do not regard them as such. Elliot Eisner has argued that what is not taught in schools is as important as what is taught.[21] A teacher who always is willing to interrupt a class discussion to lecture on the complexities of the balance of power but who refuses to "waste" class time on school rules conveys a definite message to students. It is unrealistic to expect students to gain an understanding and appreciation of rules and rule-governed behavior solely through the principal's sermons over the intercom.

> **Recommendation Number 1.3:** *Student instruction on school rules.* Students should be taught about school rules and the consequences for disobeying them.

> **Recommendation Number 1.3.1:** *Regular testing of knowledge of school rules.* Students should be tested on school rules and the consequences for disobeying them.

If students are going to be tested on school rules, it seems reasonable to make special provisions for those who demonstrate familiarity with the rules. Based on the senior author's previous experience as an administrator in a high school where students were tested annually on rules, we suggest that certain privileges be made available to students who pass their test. More will be said about such privileges in Chapter 9. Students who do not exhibit adequate knowledge of school rules or who simply refuse to take the test seriously should be denied the privileges and be placed in a mandatory review-class or study hall. When they pass the test, they too can partake of the privileges.

OTHER CURRICULUM CONSIDERATIONS

Adding content related to school rules, student values, and behavior to the regular academic curriculum is not the only way to attack discipline problems at the curricular level. Efforts should be made to eliminate boring, irrelevant subject matter and to provide opportunities for students weak in basic skills to improve themselves.

Several researchers have noted a direct relationship between poor academic performance and student behavior problems in high school.[22] School officials generally believe that most students who get into disciplinary difficulties also have learning problems.[23] Poor academic performance may be attributable to several curricular problems, including dull, irrelevant subject matter and content inappropriate to the level of student ability.

In the event that curriculum content is too hard for certain students, teachers and counselors should try to diagnose the cause of the difficulty. Some students are unable to read complex material. Others lack the problem-solving skills necessary to tackle assignments. Specialists in learning problems and remediation can be of great assistance to teachers confronted with low-achieving students. Regrettably, specialists often are unavailable at the secondary level. Though the major effort to intercept learning problems must come in elementary school, a continuing need clearly exists for intervention efforts in junior and senior high school. Any systematic attempt to reduce behavior problems at the secondary level should take into account the relationship between low achievement and behavior problems.

STUDENT INVOLVEMENT

Addressing student behavior problems through the regular academic curriculum is a vital element of the SMPSD, but this approach alone is unlikely to reduce behavior problems in schools experiencing severe disciplinary difficulties. In such situations, students must become involved in making decisions concerning their behavior and feel partially responsible for determining how to avoid further problems. Several suggestions already have been made. So far, though, nothing has been said regarding teacher behavior.

All too often, school rules pertain only to students. This fact cannot help but undermine the school's credibility as a rule-governed organization. School rules seem to exist primarily for the convenience or protection of school personnel, not students. Would it not be easier for students to respect school rules if they had some input into the process by which rules for *teacher* behavior were developed? If rules existed prohibiting teachers from embarrassing students in class and requiring teachers to return assignments promptly, students might begin to believe that rules were not solely intended for the benefit of others.

> **Recommendation Number 1.4:** *Student participation in rule-making regarding adult behavior.* Students should have opportunities to deliberate rules governing teacher behavior.

PUBLICIZING SCHOOL RULES

When rules for students and teachers are developed, they should be publicized throughout the school and community. Teaching about rules will help, but instruction may occur only once a year. Reinforcing student awareness of rules can be aided by hall posters displaying rules and the consequences for disobeying them. Annual notices of rules can be mailed to all parents. Many schools already print lists of rules in student handbooks. Perhaps local newspapers can be used as well. One novel idea for publicizing rules entails the annual involvement of students in making a film about school rules. The film could be used to stimulate community awareness and orient younger students.[24]

> **Recommendation Number 1.5:** *Frequent publicizing*

of school rules. School rules and the consequences
for disobeying them should be publicized widely and
updated regularly.

Besides publicizing school rules, special provisions should be
made for orienting students who transfer to new schools after September. With more families relocating annually, the number of students making midyear changes in schools has increased steadily.
While little systematic research has been done on the plight of the
transfer student, educators frequently observe that he or she easily
gets "lost" in new surroundings. Social isolation as well as sheer ignorance of school rules can lead to behavior problems. Care should
be taken to apprise all transfer students of school and class rules
soon after they arrive. We also recommend assigning transfer students to sympathetic advisors. The orientation of new students
should not be left up to the peer grapevine.

> **Recommendation Number 1.6:** *Orientation of trans-
> fer students.* Special arrangements should be made
> to orient all transfer students to school rules.

In one exemplary program for transfer students in Milwaukee, an
"induction center" was established for the entire city school system.
Students were placed in small classes taught by specially selected
and trained teachers. Once students manifested an adequate level of
adjustment, they were sent to regular school programs. In describing the program, Carl Byerly noted, "Behavior problems and negative attitudes were minimized if not eradicated by placing pupils in
the orientation-center classes in which they could succeed."[25]

THE NUMBER OF RULES AND RULE-ENFORCEMENT

Thus far, the suggestions have centered around student participation in rule-making and increased student awareness of rules. Other
steps can be taken, however, to improve school rules. For example,
serious consideration should be given to eliminating all nonessential
or unenforceable rules.
Lists of dozens of school rules, governing everything from chew-

ing gum to skateboards, can be as confusing for students as Internal Revenue Service regulations are for adults. In one study, investigators discovered over 100 rules and regulations in a single school![26] Few students can remember so many rules; moreover, it is unlikely that teachers can effectively enforce them. In other words, a point may be reached where the number of rules is inversely related to the capacity of school personnel for consistent enforcement.

Duke and Perry found that effective discipline policies do not necessarily depend on the presence of rules covering all possible types of misconduct. In their forementioned study of student behavior in California alternative high schools, they discovered that the presence of few rules did not result in chaos or crimewaves. Typically the only rules that existed concerned attendance and respecting the rights of others. Students participated in the development of the rules. Almost all of the eighteen schools in the sample reported few major behavior problems, particularly when compared with neighboring conventional high schools.[27]

> **Recommendation Number 1.7:** *Enforcement facilitated by minimum number of rules.* The number of school rules should be kept to a minimum in order to facilitate consistent enforcement and student retention.

The above recommendation implies that a relationship exists between student behavior and the consistency with which rules are enforced. Specialists working with young children have noted the deleterious results of inconsistent discipline at home.[28] In a very useful book on how to deal with troubled youth, Michael Rutter added that it is much easier to be consistent when rules are limited to a few meaningful ones.[29]

In schools two major varieties of inconsistency exist — "within teacher" and "between teacher." The former concerns the ability of an individual teacher to enforce the same rules consistently from one day to the next. The stories circulated by students of teachers' "good days" and "bad days" testify to the fact that students are aware of inconsistent teacher behavior. "Between teacher" inconsistency refers to the tendency within a faculty for some teachers to enforce rules while others do not. School officials who handle disciplinary referrals can attest to the fact students are quick to pick up such inconsistency and register their protest.

"Between teacher" and "within teacher" inconsistency undermine respect for the school as a rule-governed organization.[30] Teachers should not always be indicted, however; they often receive confusing messages from parents as well as school officials about what behavior is acceptable. In addition, consensus rarely exists concerning how to enforce rules. In academic matters, most parents want their children to be treated as individuals. Woe to the teacher, though, who applies the same approach to discipline. Few parents relish the idea of their children being punished while other children are not. Despite arguments in support of dealing with each behavior problem individually, many people expect rules to be applied uniformly.

We maintain that even when teachers are alert to the importance of consistent rule-enforcement, they will occasionally evidence inconsistency. Few people can act consistently all the time. For this reason, we deem it imperative for the success of the SMPSD that provisions exist for dealing constructively with instances of inconsistency. (Several general models for resolving conflicts are presented in Chapter 6.) They must provide for problem definition and negotiated solutions. Without opportunities to express concern over inconsistency and unfair discipline policies built into the school organization, it is likely that discontent will spill over into regular school activities. Students need a forum in which to voice feelings of poor treatment. Similarly, teachers need to be able to express their concerns when colleagues fail to enforce rules consistently. Any procedure designed to encourage the honest expression of dissatisfaction must ensure that those who speak are not subject to reprisals. Trust is the key to effective conflict resolution.

Besides providing opportunities to deal constructively with instances of inconsistency, school officials and teacher educators should encourage teachers to behave consistently by stressing personal influence over students. Many teachers may fail to appreciate their role as models of appropriate behavior for students. A teacher who frequently arrives late to class, enforces rules only when he or she wants to, or refuses to defend a student who has been treated unfairly by another teacher is modeling undesirable behavior.

Naturally, if school officials value consistent teacher behavior, they themselves must behave as consistently as possible. Sometimes in large schools with several administrators, however, different administrators enforce rules in varying degrees. Students learn which administrators they can manipulate and which ones to avoid. To minimize the possibility of inconsistent administrative behavior, school officials should communicate often and clearly with each other and make an effort to standardize how they handle referrals from teachers.

School officials also can encourage teachers to take greater interest in school discipline by dealing with referrals promptly. While not constrained to support a teacher when the teacher is obviously wrong, an administrator should always communicate the disposition of a referral as soon as possible. Few administrative oversights undermine a teacher's support for school rules more than neglecting to tell the teacher what action has been taken. Particularly when an administrator refuses to uphold a teacher's judgment, an effort should be made to communicate rapidly and in person with the teacher.

> **Recommendation Number 1.8:** *Procedures for consistent rule application and enforcement.* Provisions should be made for the encouragement of consistent and fair rule-enforcement and the resolution of routine problems involving inconsistencies and unfair enforcement.

CONCLUSION

Lest the previous recommendation be interpreted mistakenly as a declaration that rules are the principal reason why schools exist, we want to underscore our belief that rules are useful primarily as mechanisms for facilitating the achievement of school objectives. The existence of rules need not confirm the contention of critics that schools are just like prisons. Rules can exist to protect as well as oppress students. School rules ultimately are what those who run schools choose to make them.

For schools to be regarded as rule-governed organizations worthy of the respect of those who study and work in them, their rules must derive from and pertain to both students and school personnel. Students and teachers need to talk about rules and behavior in an open, honest way. Teachers and administrators must learn to refer to specific rules when dealing with student behavior problems and to provide every accused student with a hearing. Double standards, permitting teachers to live by one set of rules and holding students to a more harsh code of conduct, rarely are in the best interests of the school. Educators need to display the same zeal in enforcing rules related to the protection of students and their property (theft, extortion, libel, assault) as they do in enforcing attendance regulations and rules dealing with respect for authority. In other words, students need to see school rules existing for their benefit as well as the benefit of adults.

Care must be taken to deal with teacher and administrator inconsistencies promptly and constructively before they lead to student confusion and faculty morale problems. Consistent enforcement of school rules should be easier when teachers have an opportunity to participate in rule-making.

Finally, provisions should be made to include content related to all of the above subjects in the regular academic curriculum. Rules and rule-governed behavior clearly are topics worthy of study and discussion.

The recommendations in this chapter are designed to foster a school climate conducive to productive student behavior. Such an atmosphere, however, requires more than curriculum additions, greater participation in rule-making, and consistent rule-enforcement. The chapters that follow address these additional elements of the SMPSD.

Understanding the School as a Rule-Governed Organization

Recommendations:

1.1   Collaborative development of school rules.
1.2   Rules-related content incorporated in academic
        curriculum.
1.3   Student instruction on school rules.
1.3 1   Regular testing of knowledge of school rules.
1.4   Student participation in rule-making regarding
        adult behavior.
1.5   Frequent publicizing of school rules.
1.6   Orientation of transfer students.
1.7   Enforcement facilitated by minimum number of rules.
1.8   Procedures for consistent rule application
        and enforcement.

Goal Number 1: Create an awareness on the part of all who work
and study in the school that it is an organization governed by
rules.

Notes

1. Daniel L. Duke, "Looking at the School as a Rule-Governed Organization," *Journal of Research and Development in Education,* 11, 4 (Summer 1978): 116-126.
2. Gwynn Nettler, *Explaining Crime* (New York: McGraw-Hill Book Company, 1974), pp. 249-262.
3. Daniel L. Duke and Cheryl Perry, "Can Alternative Schools Succeed Where Benjamin Spock, Spiro Agnew, and B.F. Skinner Have Failed?" *Adolescence,*13, 51 (Fall 1978): 375-392.
4. James M. McPartland and Edward L. McDill, "Research on Crime in Schools" in James M. McPartland and Edward L. McDill (eds.), *Violence in Schools* (Lexington, Mass.: Lexington Books, 1977), pp. 18-19.
5. Lawrence Kohlberg, "The Cognitive-Development Approach to Moral Education," *Phi Delta Kappan,* 56, 10 (June 1975): 677.

6. "What Do You Know about Participative Decision Making?" *NASSP Bulletin,* 61, 405 (January 1977): 109.

7. Seymour Sarason, *The Culture of the School and the Problem of Change* (Boston: Allyn and Bacon, Inc., 1971), p. 175.

8. Marilyn Morissette and Albert N. Koshiyame, "Student Advocacy in School Discipline: A Look at Suspensions," *Thrust,* 6, 2 (November 1976): 17-18.

9. Thomas H. Buxton and Keith W. Prichard, "Student Perceptions of Teacher Violations of Human Rights," *Phi Delta Kappan,* 55, 1 (September 1973): 67.

10. John P. DeCecco and Arlene K. Richards, *Growing Pains: Uses of School Conflict* (New York: Aberdeen Press, 1974), p. 46.

11. U. S. Department of Health, Education and Welfare, *The Education of Adolescents,* The Final Report and Recommendation of the National Panel on High School and Adolescent Education (Washington, D.C.. U.S. Government Printing Office, 1976), p. 70.

12. Task Force '74, *The Adolescent, Other Citizens, and Their High Schools* (New York: McGraw-Hill Book Company, 1975), pp. 65-96

13. Charles F. Duff, *et al.,* "Acceptance and Rejection of Rules Governing Student Conduct," *Phi Delta Kappan,* 58, 6 (February 1977): 502: Daniel L. Duke, "How Administrators View the Crisis in School Discipline" (Stanford, 1976), p.6.

14. George H. Gallup, "Eighth Annual Gallup Poll of the Public's Attitudes Toward the Public Schools," *Phi Delta Kappan,* 58, 2 (October 1976): 189.

15. Daniel L. Duke, "Can the Curriculum Contribute to Resolving the Educator's Discipline Dilemma?" *Action in Teacher Education,* 1, 2 (Fall-Winter 1978): 17-35.

16. Developed at the University of Massachusetts, "self-sciencing" is practiced at Nueva Day School in Woodside, California. Reality therapy and "magic circles" have been described by William Glasser in *Schools Without Failure* (New York: Harper & Row, Publishers, 1969). Project TRIBES was developed by the Contra Costa Drug Education Center for use in the local school system.

17. Ralph L. Mosher and Paul R. Sullivan, "A Curriculum in Moral Education for Adolescents," *Journal of Moral Education,* 5, 2 (1976): 159-172.

18. Some of the schools' underlying ideas are discussed in Kohlberg's pre-

viously cited "The Cognitive-Developmental Approach to Moral Education."

19. Dorothy Kobak, "Teaching Children to Care," *Phi Delta Kappan,* 58, 6 (February 1977): 497.

20. Daniel L. Duke, "How Administrators View the Crisis in School Discipline," *Phi Delta Kappan,* 59, 5 (January 1978): 325-330.

21. Private communication from Elliot Eisner, School of Education, Stanford University.

22. Daniel L. Duke, "Who Misbehaves? — A High School Studies Its Discipline Problems," *Educational Administration Quarterly,* 12, 3, (Fall 1976): 65-85; Marvin Powell and Jerry Bergem, "An Investigation of the Difference Between Tenth-, Eleventh-, and Twelfth-Grade 'Conforming' and 'Nonconforming' Boys," *The Journal of Educational Research,* 56, 4 (December 1962): 184-190.

23. Daniel L. Duke, "How Administrators View the Crisis in School Discipline?"

24. Our appreciation to Richard Jung of Stanford University for this idea.

25. Carl L. Byerly, "A School Curriculum for Prevention and Remediation of Deviancy" in William W. Wattenberg (ed.), *Social Deviancy among Youth,* The Sixty-fifth Yearbook of the National Society for the Study of Education, Part I (Chicago: The University of Chicago Press, 1966), p. 251.

26. Alfred Alschuler, *et.al.,* "Social Literacy: A Discipline Game Without Losers," *Phi Delta Kappan,* 58, 8 (April 1977): 607.

27. Daniel L. Duke and Cheryl Perry, "Can Alternative Schools Succeed Where Benjamin Spock, Spiro Agenw, and B. F. Skinner Have Failed?"

28. C. G. Schoenfeld, "A Psychoanalytic Theory of Juvenile Delinquency," *Crime and Delinquency,* 17, 4 (October 1972): 475-476.

29. Michael Rutter, *Helping Troubled Children* (New York: Plenum Press, 1975), p. 147.

30. Daniel L. Duke, "Adults Can Be Discipline Problems Too!" *Psychology in the Schools,* 15, 4 (October 1978): 522-528.

5

Collecting the Data Necessary for Understanding and Improving School Discipline

Goal Number 2: Collect, maintain, and utilize data on student behavior to improve school discipline.

O SCHOOL OFFICIAL RELISHES the thought of being unaware of the behavior problems occurring in his or her school. In the previously cited study of New York and California high school administrators, in fact, over 90 percent said they routinely collected data on suspensions and truancies.[1] Over 80 percent reported collecting data on class-cutting and office referrals. Follow-up surveys revealed, however, that administrators who claimed that discipline data were kept often had difficulty putting their hands on the information. In those few schools in which data on student behavior were accessible, little evidence existed that the data were ever shared with teachers, students, or parents. Apparently, the data gathered dust on office shelves until used in the annual report to the Superintendent or the Board of Education. To be of value, data must be put to use. Data can be employed to make school personnel aware of areas in need of attention and to provide an indication of progress or lack of it. In fact, we would argue that "maintaining a system of records that provides easy access to information needed for making managerial decisions"[2] is a key component of effective management! Accurate data on student behavior are the backbone of the SMPSD.

DATA COLLECTION AND DISTRIBUTION

The goal that opens this chapter implies that data on student behavior are essential to the improvement of school discipline. To be truly useful, though, such data must be accurate and systematically collected.

> **Recommendation Number 2.1:** *Development of standard reporting procedures.* Standard procedures for reporting behavior problems should be developed.

> **Recommendation Number 2.2:** *Allocation of responsibility for data control.* One or two school employees should be given responsibility for receiving, storing, and periodically disseminating discipline data.

Unless specific procedures for data collection are spelled out and individuals designated to be in charge of the process, it is doubtful whether school officials will be in a position to know if student behavior is improving, worsening, or remaining stable. Other members of the school community should also be kept informed of student behavior. Improvements in school discipline generally require first an awareness of what the discipline problems are. Otherwise, considerable time and energy can be wasted on relatively insignificant concerns or the "pet" problems of certain individuals.

If recording and transmitting information on student behavior problems require too much time, teachers and other school personnel will refuse to cooperate. Hence, it is essential that data collection be made as efficient as possible. Standardized forms developed with input from those who must fill them out can facilitate collection and analysis of data. (See Figure 1 for a sample disciplinary referral form.)

Teacher cooperation with data-collection efforts also is contingent on feedback from school officials that their information actually is helping to reduce behavior problems. Teachers can be notified on a weekly basis, for instance, of the number and nature of student referrals to the office and of how the referrals were handled. A secretary attached to the main office staff can see to it that teachers who refer students to administrators receive feedback on any action taken. A regular agenda item at faculty meetings can be a report from a school official on trends in student behavior.

While teachers are probably the most important consumers of data on student behavior, they are not the only individuals who can benefit from a knowledge of how students are behaving. We contend that discipline is the concern of everyone in the school — students, staff, and faculty. Sharing data on student behavior minimizes the likelihood that rumors and misconceptions about discipline problems will spread. When members of the school community are aware of student behavior, they are better able to participate in rule-making and rule-enforcement activities.

On a day-to-day basis, it is critical that school officials remain abreast of student behavior problems. Others may be kept informed on a less frequent basis. In schools having several administrators who are responsible for discipline, it is all too easy to lose touch with what each individual is doing. A five-minute daily briefing before school and a slightly longer debriefing after school allow administrators to remain informed about each other's concerns. These brief meetings reduce the possibility that students or teachers will play one administrator off against another. Administrators can review any special problems they encountered since the previous meeting and divide disciplinary responsibilities as they see fit. A secretary should keep minutes of these sessions in order to facilitate any future review of disciplinary actions. Minutes also can be useful during conferences with students or parents that concern behavior problems.

> **Recommendation Number 2.3:** *Regular review of collected data.* Data on student behavior should be shared with teachers and others in the school on a regular basis. Time should be allocated so that data can be reviewed and suggestions can be made about how to improve school discipline.

One of the best ways to use raw data on student behavior to reduce discipline problems is to employ the data to establish and monitor school objectives related to behavior. Educators have been reluctant to set such objectives, despite the current concern over discipline. Objectives are created for just about every other area of school life. Why not discipline?

> **Recommendation Number 2.4:** *Functional use of data in policy making.* Data on student behavior should be used in the formulation of schoolwide objectives related to improvement in discipline.

An example may be helpful. Imagine that a high school has been receiving a number of complaints from parents and students about fighting. A review of the data on office referrals from classroom teachers, however, reveals few instances of fighting. Data from the daily summary sheets of school officials, on the other hand, indicate that a number of fights have taken place between classes, particularly near the lavatories. For one week, all school personnel are asked to exert a special effort to report any instances of aggressive behavior, inside or outside of class. At the end of the week, the data again are analyzed. The results show that most fights occur between third and fourth period, immediately prior to lunch. A task force is created by the administration. Consisting of two students, two teachers, a counselor, and an assistant principal, the task force prescribes a series of measures, including increased monitoring of the bathrooms between third and fourth period and a special "awareness clinic" after school for all students caught fighting. In addition, teachers agree to hold classroom discussions on fighting and the motives behind it. The physical education department consents to supervise boxing matches between students and to offer a course in basic self-defense for victims of aggression. Finally, the task force sets as its objective the reduction by one-half of fights among students between classes. The group convenes once a week during lunch to assess the progress of its coordinated program.

The preceding illustration demonstrates the multidimensional kind of approach that can be useful in eliminating many behavior problems and preventing their recurrence. A comprehensive campaign by the school community, rather than a piecemeal effort by a few concerned individuals, was mounted. The matter of fighting was considered important enough to merit class discussion as well as a special after-school program. An effort was made to get students to understand why fighting takes place. The potential victims of aggression, typically neglected by school officials, were provided with special training.

An important element of the program described above was that it was not dictated by the administration of the high school. Instead, representatives of several concerned groups collaborated to devise a strategy. Problem resolution based on group decision-making can help steer those who work and study in schools away from the notion that one or several individuals are responsible for solving all major problems. This kind of dependence is not in the best interests of efforts to encourage responsible behavior.

Another key aspect of the task force's campaign was the creation of a specific target-objective. Care was taken not to state the objective so that it required the complete elimination of fighting. To have done so would have created an unreal expectation, one that could not have been realized. Too often, educators set objectives based on a 100 percent change in behavior. Any adult who has tried to lose weight or quit smoking knows how difficult such expectations of perfection can be. The dieter who, having eaten a doughnut in the morning, rationalizes that his entire weight-reduction plan has been ruined and then proceeds to gorge himself for the rest of the day, exemplifies the self-defeating nature of criteria for improvement that are too rigid. Aiming for a total change in behavior can increase frustration and lead to discouragement and premature abandonment of the effort.

Yet another critical component of the task force's strategy was the provision of a thorough review of existing data on student behavior and plans for subsequent reviews of data. If the group had not made use of the information routinely collected by the office staff, it might not have realized that fighting was limited to one particular between-class period. Teacher monitors could have been deployed between all class periods, thus wasting valuable human resources. Instead, monitors were concentrated during the time when they were needed most. When a similar review of a data actually was undertaken at Lee High School in New Haven, Connecticut, school officials discovered that a significant proportion of their discipline problems took place before students reached their first class in the morning, during the hour before school when many students congregated around the locked building.[3]

Notice should be taken of the implication of the previous paragraph. A data-collection system that only covers in-class activities can miss many behavior problems. In fact, there is evidence that the behavior problems that perplex educators the most occur outside of class — on the bus, before school, between classes, in the cafeteria and restrooms, on school grounds, after school, and at dances and athletic events.[4] For this reason the system by which behavior problems are reported should be expanded to include anyone who encounters them — students, custodians, secretaries, cafeteria workers, bus drivers, and other nonteaching staff.

WHAT DATA ARE NEEDED?

Thus far the recommendations in this chapter have pertained to how to collect data on student behavior. What data should be collected is another matter. While the data needs of educators can vary from school to school, certain types of information seem to be essential for specific situations.

When the situation calls for a thorough review of school discipline in order to generate policies or develop schoolwide plans, the following types of data might be necessary:

1. Average daily attendance.
2. Average daily illegal absenteeism.
3. Average daily referrals to office.
4. Annual number of suspensions and breakdown according to reason.
5. Breakdown of number and type of student behavior problems (use Duke typology — see pages 4-5).
6. Along with above breakdowns, data on race/ethnicity of students (to determine if a disproportionate number of certain groups of students are being suspended or reported for rule-breaking).

7. Breakdown of punishments applied to students and rate of repeated offenses.
8. Estimates by administrators, counselors, and teachers of time per day spent on discipline-related matters.
9. Breakdown of student behavior problems in special programs; i.e., alternative schools, continuation schools, etc.
10. Sources of referrals to the office.
11. Comparative data on school discipline from 1) previous years and 2) nearby schools.
12. Number of student behavior problems occurring "in class" and "out of class" (before school, between classes, cafeteria, after school).
13. Number of students in disciplinary difficulty who transferred into the school after regular fall registration.

In cases involving the resolution of individual behavior problems, the following questions may need to be answered:

1. Who has disobeyed a school rule?
2. What rule was disobeyed?
3. When, where, and how was the rule disobeyed?
4. Why was the rule disobeyed?
5. Who reported the student (or other member of the school community) for disobeying the rule?
6. What action was taken?

Some of the answers to these basic questions can be provided by the person reporting the incident on a student referral form. Other questions require the accused person to respond. A hearing at which the student can answer questions and defend himself or herself is both an excellent opportunity for data collection and a basic element of the "due process" rights of any accused individual. Due process procedure includes the following components: 1) notification of charges, 2) right to counsel, 3) opportunity to rebut charges, and 4) a separation among accuser, judge, and executioner.[5] While accused students may not require legal counsel except in the most serious cases, the other provisions are important in establishing a

Figure 1

Sample Referral Form*

Date of Incident   Time   Student's Name   Grade–Class   Referred by:

Parent or Guardian: The student named above has been involved in a rule-breaking incident. The nature of the incident and the action taken are described below. Please contact the school official who signed the report for additional information.

Rule-Breaking Incident
___ Tardy to class
___ Disrupting class
___ Fighting
___ Unexcused absence
___

Action Taken
___ Student conference
___ Referral to counselor
___ Conference with student & teacher
___ Parent conference
___

Sanction
___ Issuance of Warning
___ After-school detention
___ Reimbursement for damage
___ Suspension for ___ days
___

*The form should be printed in three copies — parent, office and teacher's copies. It can be printed so that it fits into a standard, legal-sized envelope.

climate that reinforces the notion that the school is a rule-governed organization.

In schools with significant amounts of out-of-class behavior problems, it may be useful to employ blueprint layouts of the school building and grounds for data-collection purposes. Instances of rule-breaking behavior can then be pinpointed, in much the same fashion that police maintain "crime maps" of city neighborhoods. If certain areas become the scenes of frequent misconduct, school officials may wish to provide greater supervision or consider environmental redesign.

When the immediate purpose of data-collection is to devise a corrective strategy for a particular student, the questions that may be asked take on a slightly different tone from those that may be employed at a hearing or on a referral form. Marc Robert adapted a series of useful questions from the work of William Glasser:

1. What did you (the student) do?
   This establishes the circumstances of the situation and clarifies the student's responsibility.
2. Did it help you?
   The student evaluates his own actions.
3. Can you make a plan? Can we make a plan together?
4. Will you carry out the plan?
5. Did you do what you said you would do?[6]

Certain kinds of disciplinary data can be of special significance to school officials. In light of recent court rulings regarding student suspensions and expulsions, detailed records should be kept each time such actions are taken. As concern builds that suspensions and expulsions serve little educational function and that they are applied disproportionately to minority students, school officials are being called on to justify as well as document their policies.[7]

The increase of crime and violence in schools has drawn the attention of outsiders to school affairs. Legislators and law enforcement officials request specific data on the extent to which unlawful activities occur in schools. School officials may not be prepared to respond to these requests, however. In a recent survey, Duke was surprised to discover that approximately 25 percent of the administrators who responded said they maintained no systematic records on criminal activity in their schools.[8]

Besides keeping data on student activities of a criminal nature, school officials may find it valuable to have ready access to the following kinds of information:

1. Which students are not assigned to class during any particular period?
2. Which students have permission to arrive late or leave early?
3. Which students are engaged in extracurricular activities or are on field trips?
4. Which students participate in work-study programs or are involved in independent study assignments that permit them to leave campus?

Answers to these and similar questions should help school officials verify reports that students are missing class. Criminal activities involving students during school hours typically occur when students should be in class.

On a daily basis, school personnel naturally need to know which students are absent from school. Such data are not only required by law; they permit school officials to monitor attendance trends and check on students who are reported to be absent, but who linger around school. Increasing numbers of students are being reported for coming to school but not attending homeroom or classes. Since these students frequently get into trouble or cause other students to misbehave, school officials should be aware of them.

School absenteeism is receiving considerable publicity. Parents worry that their children leave home but do not reach school. School officials are concerned about loss of revenue. Teachers become demoralized when students who miss school drop far behind the rest of the class. Police officials worry that young people who are not in school too easily become involved in illegal acts. To facilitate school efforts to monitor student attendance routine procedures for contacting parents and verifying absences should be implemented. Often such procedures exist, but are not followed regularly. Employing parent or student volunteers can be useful in bolstering the efforts of school personnel to maintain home contact.

A written record of each phone call should be kept. For better or worse, this is the Age of Liability as far as school personnel are concerned. Without records indicating that attempts were made to check on students reported as absent, school officials may find themselves subject to charges of negligence. A number of helpful tips on how to collect records on absentees and improve school attendance are contained in a recent pamphlet entitled "Where Have All the Students Gone?" and distributed by the National PTA.

In Oakland, California, the Superintendent and school district personnel recently embarked on a major campaign to reduce illegal absenteeism. By developing standard reporting procedures, hiring clerks to assist in daily telephoning both during and after school, and offering participating schools the incentive of a percentage of the money saved at each school site, the district reported a savings of $42,000 in ADA (Average Daily Attendance) funds for the month of February 1979 alone.

OTHER HELPFUL DATA

Not all data of value in improving school discipline pertains specifically to behavior problems such as truancy and criminal activity. Information on study habits, academic progress, and classroom attitudes may assist teachers and counselors in detecting the onset of problems. Problems with schoolwork often lead to behavior problems.

An example of the kind of data that may be useful are teacher impressions of student progress while doing seatwork. Armed with a clipboard and a student checklist, a teacher can circulate among students, noting how much work each student has accomplished and any instances of off-task behavior. If the student has not made any progress by the next time seatwork is assigned, the teacher knows instantly and can initiate corrective actions. Such routine datagathering prevents teachers with dozens of students from losing track of particular individuals during individualized instruction or independent study assignments. Teachers also can use their daily "jottings" to buttress recommendations made during teacher-student or teacher-parent conferences.

So far the suggestions for what data to collect have been limited largely to descriptive information. When decisions must be made about how best to help students or how to modify the curriculum or instructional plan to deal with changing student behavior, explanatory data may be required as well.

Counselors generally keep anecdotal records and test results that can assist in explaining why students may currently be experiencing difficulties. Although these data can be of benefit, the quality and reliability of such information varies widely. Numerous instruments are available to help educators predict which students are likely to have various kinds of problems. Unfortunately, using predictive instruments can backfire, occasioning the much-mentioned "self-fulfilling prophecy." In other words, students whose data profiles suggest that they are more likely to experience problems may be treated in ways that ensure they do! Witness the student identified as a potential delinquent who begins to be treated with such suspicion by his teachers that he develops a low self-image and starts behaving in a deviant manner.

Instead of relying on predictive instruments and anecdotal records, educators should be prepared to gather as much data as possible at the first sign that a student is having academic or behavioral problems in school. Such information can be collected relatively efficiently in a faculty troubleshooting session or case conference, both of which are discussed in Chapter 6. Asking students to discuss their problems also can provide valuable clues to account for changes in behavior.

DATA AND PUBLIC RELATIONS

Besides assisting in the identification and treatment of individual student problems and the development of schoolwide disciplinary policies, data on student behavior can be useful in refuting unconstructive rumors.[9] School officials know that how students behave is a topic of great local interest. People speculate on the extent to which students break rules and why. Parents frequently base their judgments of school effectiveness on how they feel students behave in school. Schools are fishbowls. People driving or walking past a school sometimes assume that the presence of a few students furtively smoking behind a tree or stealing away from campus bespeak a general state of disorder. Impressions gleaned in this way by taxpayers and passed on by word-of-mouth easily can undermine community support for education. It is therefore critical that data not only be collected regarding student behavior and achievement, but that data be used whenever possible to correct erroneous public impressions.

One illustration of the usefulness of data in correcting public misconceptions related to school discipline was provided in a recent report on mandated desegregation in a suburban community.[10] Contrary to the popular belief that integration creates problems by heightening tensions between whites and nonwhites, the report documented how "behavioral incidents" actually declined over the four years of the integration experiment. Not only did student conduct improve, so did student achievement. The authors of the report concluded:

Through a systematic use of evaluative studies, Forrestville (a pseudonym) is identifying and moving toward solutions to (its) problems. As a consequence, community instability, white flight, and parent dissatisfaction with the schools have receded during the four years of integration. Equally important, Forrestville schools have solid data that they are improving achievement and attitudes toward learning among all students.[11]

The lesson of Forrestville for school officials is clear: never underestimate the importance of facts in disspelling erroneous assumptions about education.

Instead of waiting for rumors to mushroom and then presenting "the facts" to the public, school officials should consider regularly disseminating data. In addition, if educators expect the public to believe the information they are given, educators must be willing to acknowledge the bad along with the good. We maintain that it is preferable for school officials to admit when they are experiencing problems and invite community assistance rather than to conceal disappointing data, thereby attempting to create the impression of a trouble-free organization.

> **Recommendation Number 2.5:** *Public reporting of discipline data.* Data on school discipline should be reported regularly to the Board of Education and the general public.

School officials realize that members of the Board of Education are likely to receive gossip and complaints related to school discipline. Rather than keeping Board members guessing about student behavior, we advocate informing them regularly about suspensions, attendance patterns, and trends in classroom conduct. Not only is the sharing of such data consistent with the notion of open government; it is sound administrative policy. Informed Board members can be powerful allies of school officials, helping to quell rumors and devise plans of action.

At times it also may be appropriate to apprise local news media of discipline-related matters. School officials should not presume that parents are uninterested in student behavior, nor should they feel that parents do not deserve such information. Parents care about the place to which they send their children five days a week.

In the event that local news media thrive on sensationalism and distortions of school events, it may be necessary to utilize alternatives, such as a school newsletter. Using a school-published newsletter, however, should not become an opportunity to control the flow of information. Honest admission of problems may not stimulate greater public support or win a budget election, but it is the only conscientious choice. If school officials are not moved toward open disclosure for ethical reasons, they may at least be influenced by public outrage as over the Watergate crisis.

Before concluding this section on the importance of collecting data on student behavior and using it to improve school discipline, we must sound a note of caution. Referring again to the Watergate scandals, it was revealed at the time of the investigations that the White House had amassed great quantities of data on its "enemies." School officials should not view students as adversaries about whom to collect incriminating evidence. Richard Nixon and his cohorts seem to have regarded data as more valuable for punishing individuals than for improving conditions. The information that school officials collect on student behavior is privileged. The students to whom the information pertains have rights under the Constitution. Confidentiality should be guarded at all times. As one precaution against "data abuse," information may be classified according to type of problem, date of problem, or disposition of problem rather than student name. *Under no circumstances should any public reports of student behavior data include references to specific individuals.*

Data are no better than the uses to which they are put. The functional uses of data are dependent on the kinds of people who have access to the data. It is imperative that those who work with disciplinary data realize the information on student behavior is intended for the improvement of school discipline and the betterment of the school's climate for learning.

Collecting the Data Necessary for Understanding and Improving School Discipline

Recommendations:

2.1 Development of standard reporting procedures.
2.2 Allocation of responsibility for data control.
2.3 Regular review of collected data.
2.4 Functional use of data in policy making.
2.5 Public reporting of discipline data.

Goal Number 2: Collect, maintain, and utilize data on student behavior to improve school discipline.

Notes

1. Daniel L. Duke, "How Administrators View the Crisis in School Discipline," *Phi Delta Kappan,* 59, 5 (January 1978).

2. Elizabeth G. Cohen, Jo-Ann K. Intili, and Susan H. Robbins, "Task and Authority: A Sociological View of Classroom Management" in Daniel L. Duke, *Classroom Management,* The Seventy-Eighth Yearbook of the National Society for the Study of Education, Part II (Chicago: The University of Chicago Press, 1979), p. 129.

3. Robert Schreck, *et al.,* "The Metamorphosis of Lee High School," *Urban Education,* 10, 2 (July 1975): 203.

4. Daniel L. Duke and Adrienne M. Meckel, "Disciplinary Roles in American Schools" (submitted for publication).

5. John P. DeCecco and Arlene K. Richards, *Growing Pains: Uses of School Conflict,* New York: Aberdeen Press, 1974, pp. 78-79.

6. Marc Robert, *Loneliness in the Schools* (Niles, Illinois: Argus Communications, 1973), pp. 118-119.

7. George Neill, "Control Spector Hovers as HEW Requests Detailed Reports on Discipline Measures," *Phi Delta Kappan,* 57, 4 (December 1975): 286-287.

8. Daniel Duke, "How Administrators View the Crisis in School Discipline."

9. Walter D. St. John, "Dealing with Problem Situations," *NASSP Bulletin,* 61, 405 (January 1977): 47.

10. Maurice J. Eash and Sue Pinzur Rasher, "Mandated Desegregation and Improved Achievement: A Longitudinal Study," *Phi Delta Kappan,* 58, 5 (January 1977): 394-397.

11. *Ibid.,* p. 397.

6

Expanding the School's Conflict-Resolution Capacity

Goal Number 3: Provide opportunities for those who work and study in school to express their concerns and problems in a supportive atmosphere.

A BASIC ASSUMPTION UNDERLYING THE SMPSD is that conflict in schools is unavoidable. Not all conflicts related to student behavior are *caused* by students. Many result from inconsistencies, misperceptions or poor teaching on the part of school personnel. Since it may be difficult to understand the etiology and magnitude of a behavior problem from a student referral form, mechanisms that permit all parties to a conflict to be heard are important. Such mechanisms, be they conferences with teachers and students or structured negotiations between the administration and student body, can resolve problems before they escalate into major upsets. Ten minutes of reasoned deliberation after class between a teacher and a student accused of misconduct sometimes can prevent a transient concern from becoming a fullblown crisis, replete with hurt feelings, lingering animosity, and continued behavior problems.

To bypass prompt, face-to-face conflict resolution between accused and accuser is to risk undermining the educator's personal effectiveness and to deny the students their basic rights. Rarely should immediate punishment or the referral of a student elsewhere be a teacher's first response to a behavior problem.

RESOLVING CONFLICTS IN CLASS

Most conflicts between teachers and students can and should be handled at the classroom level. We advise teachers attempting conflict-resolution procedures to deal exclusively with the immediate problem. General discussions of past problems or the student's personality shift the focus away from reaching an effective decision concerning the immediate situation. Accused students may feel the purpose of such interactions is to attack them or get revenge, rather than to improve behavior.

> **Recommendation Number 3.1:** *Situation specificity.* In any process of conflict-resolution in school, educators should attempt to deal only with the specific situation at hand.

Recommending that a conflict be handled in a situation-specific manner sounds simpler than it actually is. To filter out previous contacts with students is often difficult. Many believe that previous knowledge of an individual is useful in dealing with current concerns. If the objective is improved behavior, however, the focus clearly must be on the present problem. Handling discipline problems at the classroom rather than the administrative level will help keep this focus.

If the teacher handles his or her own conflicts rather than referring them elsewhere, the likelihood will be greater that behavior problems will not mushroom into major concerns. Accused students who have to wait for an appointment with an administrator or counselor often grow disgruntled and feel ignored. Sometimes these feelings gave rise to the misconduct in the first place! The longer a problem must wait to be confronted and resolved, the greater the chance it will also be recalled inaccurately by one or both parties involved. In addition, the longer a student must wait to get a hearing, the less likely he or she will be able to devote attention to current academic tasks.

Besides these practical considerations, some ethical reasons call for resolving conflicts as swiftly as possible. Students who are accused of improper behavior deserve to be informed of the charges as soon as possible, preferably by the accusing individual. In turn, the accuser should provide the student with an opportunity (hearing) to explain his or her actions. The Supreme Court has acknowledged that students do not shed their constitutional rights when they enter school.

> **Recommendation Number 3.2:** *Speedy action necessary.* Conflicts that arise in the classroom should be handled between the teacher and the student(s) involved as soon after they occur as possible.

> **Recommendation Number 3.2.1:** *Private conferences.* Conflict-resolution procedures should take place on an individual basis and in private.

> **Recommendation Number 3.2.2.:** *Informational hearings.* Students accused of misconduct should have an opportunity (hearing) to explain how they perceive what occurred and why.

> **Recommendation Number 3.2.3.:** *Negotiated problem-solving.* Solutions to conflicts should be negotiated between teacher and student(s).

For many teachers, the preceding recommendations may sound logical but impractical, given their teaching schedules. Is a teacher expected to interrupt class and go into the hall for a conflict-resolution session? Should he or she ask a student to wait until after class or come during lunch period? Providing time to meet individually with students experiencing behavior problems is a critical dimension of any conflict-resolution scheme; but it is impossible to prescribe a single, foolproof way to rearrange class time. Some teachers have access to teacher aides or volunteers, thus enabling them to leave class when the need arises. Others work in teams that facilitate spontaneous conflict resolution. Teachers who individualize instruction may find they can more easily deal with problems as they arise than their colleagues who rely on large-group instruction. The latter group may have to meet with students between classes, during preparation periods, or after school. Where modifications in the physical nature of the self-contained classroom are possible, it may be helpful to construct a small conference area with a window to permit the teacher to hold a private meeting without losing sight of the other students. In any event, it is critical that teachers recognize that the time required to listen to students and resolve conflicts is time well spent.

No simple formula exists for transforming teachers who regard listening to students as a waste of instructional time into individuals who realize the value of such activity. Perhaps workshops in which teachers and students are free to discuss ways to handle their concerns can serve as a first step. Students candidly admit to feelings of being ignored. In one study of ninth graders, over half the students expressed a desire to have someone to talk to about their problems at school.[1] An unfortunate truism in most schools is that one of the scarcest commodities for students is someone to listen to them. Young people are surrounded at home, school, and elsewhere with adults who have things to say to them, but little time to hear what the young have to say. Small wonder that resentment builds!

In their studies of democratic dilemmas faced by young people, DeCecco and Richards discovered that adults in schools are perceived as trying to control student emotions by restricting their verbal expression. The authors admonish educators that "banning verbal expression of emotions, particularly anger . . . . increases the likelihood that unverbalized emotion will control behavior."[2]

Teachers may do well to reflect on how they themselves feel when no one gives them a chance to explain their feelings. Complaints from teacher organizations to administrators and central office personnel indicate that teachers, like students, often feel that no one is listening. Perhaps asking teachers to role-play students can help raise the consciousness level of those who find it difficult to see the value of people who are willing to listen as well as instruct. Other useful techniques for building empathy and understanding have come out of the human potential movement, sensitivity training, and affective education.

One way to facilitate the process of getting teachers to spend more time listening to students is to revise the organizational expectations for teachers. The developers of Individually Guided Education accomplished this task by specifying that all teachers should also serve as student advisors. Time is set aside for teachers to listen to student concerns and assist in locating solutions. Research on student behavior in alternative high schools confirms the fact that behavior problems can be minimized in settings where students feel they have ready access to teachers who are disposed to listen.[3]

Administrators naturally share some responsibility for providing the structural support that will free teachers for regular conference periods with students during the school day. Administrators might offer their services as short-term substitutes for a few minutes each day in order that teachers could schedule counseling appointments with their students. Schools that have long-term substitutes assigned to them (as do some schools in California), might arrange for a regular "spelling" of teachers by the substitutes on days when the latter are not scheduled for full-time substitute duty. Administrators thus can encourage speedy hearings for students with behavioral, academic or personal concerns.

HELPING TEACHERS LISTEN

A variety of approaches to classroom management stress the importance of good teacher-student communications, including prompt, situation-specific conflict resolution. Haim Ginott, Ken Ernst, and Thomas Gordon all have suggested that many classroom behavior problems arise as a result of the way teachers talk to students.[4]

Ginott advocated "congruent communication," by which he meant communication that is harmonious and authentic. Words should fit feelings. Too often, he claimed, teachers underestimate the power of the words they use. Simply because students do not appear to pay attention in class does not mean they are unaware of what teachers are saying. Among the tips Ginott offered those desiring to improve classroom communications are the following:

1. Examine how you respond to students.
2. Communicate acceptance rather than rejection, even when dealing with problems.
3. Address yourself to the student's situation rather than judge his character and personality.
4. Express anger without insult.
5. Avoid diagnosing or labeling students, sarcasm, hurried help, lengthy sermons, phony supportiveness, and too much praise.
6. When praising, praise specific acts rather than character traits.

Thomas Gordon's best-selling book *T.E.T.: Teacher Effectiveness Training* echoed Ginott's suggestions while prescribing a more precise approach to the resolution of classroom conflicts. Gordon urged teachers to refrain from thinking about settling disputes in terms of winners and losers. When conflicts arise, he recommended these negotiation procedures:

1. Teacher and student meet privately to discuss the problem at hand.
2. They determine whether the student's perception of the problem corresponds to the teacher's.
3. The teacher and student generate possible solutions to the problem.
4. Teacher and student eliminate solutions unacceptable to either and mutually agree to try a solution satisfactory to both.
5. Teacher and student determine how and when the solution will be implemented.
6. If necessary, teacher and student meet again to assess how well the plan is working.

Imagine that a problem has arisen concerning Billy's answering out of turn in class. Rather than imposing a punishment on Billy, the teacher asks him to drop by after class. Using "I" statements and sticking to the specific problem at hand, the teacher indicates that talking out of turn has become a problem. Billy then has an opportunity to explain his actions without any judgments being made about his worth as a person. By following the steps in the negotiation process, the teacher and Billy work through the problem collaboratively. This joint approach is quite unlike the typical way problems are resolved in class. Traditionally, students have learned to depend exclusively on the teacher to impose a settlement. The process by which teachers (or other school personnel) always come up with a solution to conflicts all but assures, to Gordon, "that students will remain helplessly dependent, immature, infantile."[5] He goes further to contend,

The greatest disservice teachers perform for students is rushing in to protect youngsters from their problems, thus denying them a crucial experience: dealing with the consequences of their own solutions.[6]

Ken Ernst's application of Eric Berne's Transactional Analysis to classroom problems overlaps many of the ideas of Ginott and Gordon. He maintains that the words expressed by teachers and students are more than public communications; they also are indicators of ulterior motives and repressed feelings. To ignore this "hidden" content or fail to appreciate the significance of verbal transactions in class is to reduce the teacher's effectiveness in dealing with student behavior.

Though the three references cited above prescribe somewhat different approaches to the resolution of classroom conflicts, they share a common emphasis on the quality of communications between students and teachers. The writers minimize the importance of such popular classroom-management devices as rewards, punishments, exciting learning materials, and inspirational teaching techniques.

Each of the three approaches is based on the belief that no substitute exists for patience and careful listening. Teachers are urged to abandon their expectations that problems can be handled quickly and efficiently and to overcome the attitude that "If at first you don't succeed, quit." Rather than giving up on students who fail to respond the way they are expected to respond, teachers should model persistence, while continuing to keep open channels of communication. Such behavior, although requiring more time and understanding, communicates at a nonverbal level that teachers *care* about students. Otherwise, students receive the message that all a teacher really cares about is finishing what he or she planned to do.

It can also help for teachers to view certain behaviors — such as talking out of turn, refusing to cooperate, and engaging in off-task activities — as *opportunities* rather than *problems*. Often these behaviors serve as indirect ways by which students communicate their upsets. Teachers need to know such information if they are to maximize their effectiveness.

WHEN PROBLEMS OUTGROW THE CLASSROOM

Despite the recommendations in the first part of this chapter, we consider it naive to think that all student behavior problems can be resolved at the classroom level. Certain nonnegotiable problems, such as possession of dangerous weapons, drug use, and assault, require the involvement of school officials and, on occasion, police authorities. Other problems, including poor attendance and disrespect for authority, may be open to negotiation, but not between teacher and student. Opportunities should be available for all parties to a problem to present their cases. Obviously, if a student admits to disobeying a rule and there are no extenuating circumstances, recourse to conflict-resolution procedures is unnecessary. Only when a student feels that he has been unjustly accused should these procedures be utilized.

> **Recommendation Number 3.3:** *Trained resource persons.* When conflicts cannot be resolved at the classroom level between teacher and student, resource people should be available to hear both sides of the issue and assist in negotiating a settlement.

> **Recommendation Number 3.3.1:** *Collaborative selection of resource persons.* In order for the resource persons to enjoy maximum credibility, students and teachers should be involved in their selection.

Recommendation Number 3.3.2: *Impartial functioning of resource persons.* A resource person should regard his or her primary functions as 1) providing a hearing for the conflicting parties and 2) negotiating a solution to the conflict that is acceptable to them. Under no circumstances should he or she serve as an agent of the administration concerned with enforcing school rules or meting out punishments.

Accessibility to persons who will listen to students experiencing problems is a major organizational concern that must be confronted before any conflict-resolution process can be truly effective. Where teachers are too tightly scheduled to be able to meet with students, it may be necessary to utilize supporting staff—counselors, school officials not involved in discipline, the school nurse, or resource teachers. Chapter 11 contains additional remarks on the allocation of time in schools.

Time is not the only factor to consider when planning conflict-resolution procedures. Space also is important. "Neutral turf" is more desirable than locations associated with discipline or punishment. Some school officials open the cafeteria each morning before school. During this time an administrator is available to hear complaints and concerns from students.[7] One California school schedules a counselor in a small exercise-room, equipped with weights, where students come freely to discuss their concerns while they exercise away their frustrations. Where students are unwilling or unable to come to school, "outreach" programs may be useful. Schools can provide inducements to counselors or popular teachers to "set up shop" in the community, perhaps occupying someone's apartment or a secondhand van. Occasionally students are so busy during school hours or so reluctant to wait in a line outside the guidance office that they may not receive the attention they need. After-school or evening hours for counselors, either at school or in the community, can be an important supplement to the guidance program of a school and a vital element of the conflict-resolution process.[8]

So far we have operated on the assumption that existing school personnel can be utilized as student advisors, conflict resolvers, and sources of support for troubled individuals. In many schools, however, counselors already are burdened with large caseloads; and teachers lack free time. In such instances it may prove helpful to employ a conflict-resolution specialist. Community liaisons are used in some districts. Others have adopted the role of ombudsman.[9]

An ombudsman is an individual whose fulltime responsibility involves hearing complaints and suggesting ways to solve them. The role is based on the belief that other organizational members — in this case teachers and counselors — are too closely identified with "the system" to be truly effective in dealing with many problems. An ombudsman receives gripes and redirects them to the appropriate people, usually eliminating much of the red tape that the complaining party might encounter while protecting his or her identity. Since people know what the ombudsman is supposed to do, they tend to be less threatened when he or she transmits a complaint. Providing such a person to hear personal concerns often reduces the likelihood that they will remain unresolved for long periods of time, thus undermining morale and productivity.

STUDENT INVOLVEMENT IN CONFLICT RESOLUTION

Despite the neutrality of an ombudsman or the cordiality of a respected teacher-advisor, occasions may arise when no adult can be trusted to hear a problem or participate in its resolution. In such situations it seems desirable to involve students in the conflict-resolution process.

> **Recommendation Number 3.4:** *Student participation in problem-solving.* Opportunities should be provided for students to participate in the conflict-resolution process.

Typically, if students are involved in school discipline at all, they serve as members of a student court. School officials sometimes report that students do not take their court responsibilities seriously, that they mete out unduly harsh punishments, and that they rarely are obeyed by those who get into trouble most frequently.[10] Another problem with student courts is that they generally are staffed by relatively few students. Students who do not have a chance to serve often look on the court as yet another exclusive "club" like student government.

The fact that student courts have not been reported to be particularly effective does not mean that they might not be a valuable component of the SMPSD. In a few locations, such as Lexington, Kentucky, student courts have received praise for their efficient handling of peer discipline.[11] In Denver, a countywide peer court has been established to handle nonviolent cases. Individuals brought before the peer court instead of a juvenile court judge must admit guilt and agree to accept the contractual arrangements made by the seven-student panel. In writing about Soviet schools, Uric Bronfenbrenner has observed that student tribunals generally handle all student behavior problems.[12] The only time a teacher becomes involved is when he or she feels the sentence handed down by the court is too harsh. Such a practice casts the teacher in a totally different light. Instead of serving as a policeman and a punisher, the teacher is free to function as a student advocate, speaking up only when it is necessary to reduce a penalty.

What the Kentucky, Colorado and Soviet experiences suggest is that educators need not take for granted that the adolescent peer group must inevitably act as a negative influence on behavior, striving always to "beat the system" and establish its own anti-adult norms. Perhaps educators should begin to consider seriously the positive roles that students can play in monitoring their own behavior. Participation on student courts clearly is one possibility. A second alternative involves students in the role of peer counselor.

One of the most publicized peer counseling programs in the United States is located in Palo Alto, California.[13] Largely the inspiration of Barbara Varenhorst, the Palo Alto Peer Counseling Program (PAPCP) is open to all secondary students willing to devote 18 hours of time to being trained. The training takes place in small groups and entails the following topics:

I.   Communication Skills (4 weeks)
     A. Verbal one-to-one conversation
     B. Behavioral communication
     C. Communication with a small group of peers who are
        strangers
     D. Large-group communication
II. Decision-Making Applied to Working on Common Problems
     (4 weeks)
     A. Family difficulties
     B. Peer relationships
     C. School problems (being a new student, cliques, etc.)
     D. Health (drugs, physical handicaps, etc.)
III. Ethics and Strategies of Counseling (4 weeks)
     A. What is counseling?
     B. Potential resources for peer counselors
     C. Limitations and potentials of the peer counselor role
     D. Getting started, confidentiality, and records.

The PAPCP seems to be based on the belief that adolescents need occasions during their development when they can communicate with each other in an open, honest way. Knowing grammar and having a good vocabulary do not ensure that young people can send or receive messages effectively. Peer counseling offers an opportunity for the young to communicate concerning meaningful concerns. Peer counselors receive referrals from teachers and guidance counselors. Each request for assistance must have a clear problem-statement together with the type of assistance desired. One peer counselor may be asked to try and reduce a student's aggressive behavior. Another may be invited to participate in a district-wide research study by interviewing students about sensitive issues.

Assessing the impact of the PAPCP, Varenhorst reported that changes were noted in the behavior of both peer counselors and counselees. Parents as well as teachers observed these positive changes. Students seemed to function better in group situations, and the entire school climate was perceived to have improved.

CRISIS INTERVENTION AND NEGOTIATIONS

No matter how well students and teachers learn to communicate with each other and despite the availability of various resource people, both students and adults, it is safe to predict that certain problems will periodically require additional efforts. When Lee High School in New Haven, Connecticut, faced escalating behavior problems related to racial tensions, for example, the following set of procedures was developed to defuse conflicts and guide administrative intervention:

1. Remove conflicting parties to a private area where they do not feel pressure to "perform" in order to "save face."
2. Separate the combatants and provide them with an opportunity to diffuse their momentary emotions.
3. Elicit from the separated belligerents all of the facts leading up to the incident.
4. Establish ground rules that will govern a meeting of the belligerent parties.
5. Bring the conflicting parties together and repeat the ground rules to assure a controlled presentation of the basic problem.
6. Keep the presentation focused on the facts and issues of the situation.
7. Repeat the factual accounts to the participants making certain that there is basic agreement on the facts and areas of disagreement.
8. Suggest alternative methods of resolving the issue.
9. Encourage both parties to decide on an acceptable alternative likely to prevent further disagreement.
10. Secure commitments from both parties that, in the event of further pressures for "renewed hostilities," such pressures would be brought to the attention of the administrators who negotiated the settlement of the original incident.[14]

A value of this ten-step strategy is that it represents a consistent and systematic approach to conflict resolution, one that means school officials no longer appear to be caught off guard without a reasonable course of action. Too often, educators only exacerbate matters by reacting hastily to an unanticipated crisis. The existence of a contingency plan may spell the difference between manageable conflict and complete disorder.

The crisis-intervention scheme developed at Lee High School served the purpose of demonstrating to students a positive model by which problems could be addressed in the future. As the authors of the Lee High School study concluded:

The educative process of teaching adolescents to resolve problems around a conference table replaced the conventional approach of "throwing out the troublemakers.[15]

An alternative to the model developed at Lee High School has been provided by John DeCecco and Arlene Richards. Acknowledging the positive value of "dissent in a supportive environment" and "the open verbal expression of anger," they recommend a three-part negotiations model:

1. The statement of issues by each side made with direct, verbal expression of anger.
2. Agreement by all sides on a common statement of issues (agreeing to disagree).
3. Bargaining in which each side makes concessions.[16]

In order to get conflicting parties to negotiate, a mediator sometimes is needed. Mediators should be acceptable to all parties and personally uninvolved in the dispute. Initially they may have to listen to each side separately, but the eventual goal of a mediator is to bring those in disagreement together for face-to-face discussion.

DeCecco and Richards feel that their negotiations model is particularly well-suited to problems that might involve groups of students — for example, racial friction following school integration efforts. They express the belief that

The act of negotiation is one of both love and sacrifice. First, it requires school adults to sacrifice the time and trouble to listen to the angry complaints of students. It shows students that adults care enough for them to listen even though they often rebel. Second, it requires adults to share and give up some power. This sacrifice also shows that adults care enough to go through the pain of negotiation.[17]

CRISIS TEACHERS

Negotiations are not always possible or appropriate for resolving conflicts involving students. Sometimes a crisis teacher, crisis team, or crisis-intervention center may be better equipped to deal with problem behavior. Stanley Sanders and Janis Yarbrough have contended that a majority of any school's serious behavior problems are caused by a very small percentage of students.[18] These students typically require the presence of an individual or group of people to whom they can be referred for special, short-term instruction (rather than punishment). The idea is that students experiencing episodic bouts of unconstructive behavior may benefit more from a brief placement in a highly structured setting than from traditional disciplinary action. While in the "crisis" referral setting, the students can express their upsets while continuing to work on their regular class assignments. Thus, they experience no significant break in the continuity of their academic work. New York State has established the Comprehensive Support Service Program (CSSP) to provide special teachers for ongoing intervention with troubled students. Working in conjunction with regular teachers, CSSP specialists help plan and conduct programs for students with behavioral problems or learning disabilities.

Adults who are selected to serve in a crisis-intervention capacity obviously need special skills and personality characteristics. A knowledge of how to deal with learning and behavior problems and counseling skills are critical. Patience, understanding, and eventemperedness also are important.

A FINAL NOTE

It is doubtful that conflict-resolution procedures will work well in schools where administrators and teachers are reluctant to deal with students as individuals entitled to respect and equal protection under the law. Personal observations of schools where discipline problems abound and of schools where students and teachers coexist harmoniously have convinced us that no substitute exists for educators who are compassionate and genuinely interested in students. Arbitrary, authoritative resolution of student problems by educators undermines a climate of caring and encourages students to "beat the system." By sharing authority for conflict resolution, educators demonstrate their belief that most students can act responsibly and in a manner consistent with the development of good citizenship. As a result, the handling of student behavior problems becomes an element of the school's total learning program.

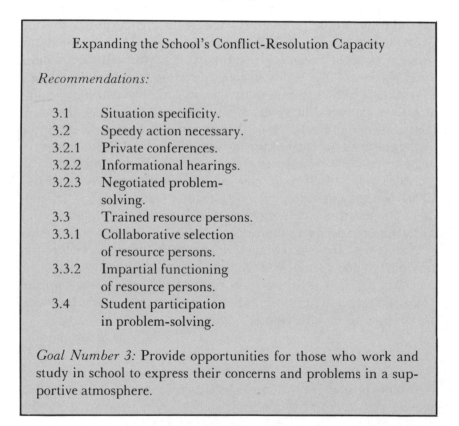

Expanding the School's Conflict-Resolution Capacity

Recommendations:

3.1	Situation specificity.
3.2	Speedy action necessary.
3.2.1	Private conferences.
3.2.2	Informational hearings.
3.2.3	Negotiated problem-solving.
3.3	Trained resource persons.
3.3.1	Collaborative selection of resource persons.
3.3.2	Impartial functioning of resource persons.
3.4	Student participation in problem-solving.

Goal Number 3: Provide opportunities for those who work and study in school to express their concerns and problems in a supportive atmosphere.

Notes

1. Karl C. Garrison and Ben W. Cunningham, "Personal Problems of Ninth-Grade Pupils," *The School Review,* 60, 1 (January 1952): 33.

2. John P. DeCecco and Arlene K. Richards, *Growing Pains: Uses of School Conflict* (New York: Aberdeen Press), p.88.

3. Daniel L. Duke and Cheryl Perry, "Can Alternative Schools Succeed Where Benjamin Spock, Spiro Agnew, and B. F. Skinner Have Failed?" *Adolescence,* 13, 51 (Fall 1978): 378-392.

4. Haim G. Ginott, *Teacher & Child* (New York: Avon Books, 1972); Ken Ernst, *Games Students Play* (Millbrae, California: Celestial Arts, 1975); and Thomas Gordon, *T.E.T.: Teacher Effectiveness Training* (New York: Peter W. Wyden, Publisher, 1974).

5. Thomas Gordon, *T.E.T.: Teacher Effectiveness Training,* p.8.

6. *Ibid.,* p. 111.

7. Robert Schreck, *et al.* "The Metamorphosis of Lee High School," *Urban Education,* 10, 2 (July 1975): 204.

8. Henry Zacharias Rosner, "Three Practices to Reach Students," *Personnel and Guidance Journal,* 53, 1 (September 1974): 65-67.

9. A description of the ombudsman's functions is included in "Crusader for Conciliation?" *Nation's Schools,* 89, 6 (June 1972): 33-38.

10. Evidence of the lack of popularity of student courts can be found in the previously cited study entitled "How Administrators View the Crisis in School Discipline."

11. *The Education of Adolescents,* The Final Report and Recommendations of the National Panel on High School and Adolescent Education (Washington, D.C.: U.S. Government Printing Office, 1976), p. 74.

12. Urie Bronfenbrenner, *Two Worlds of Childhood: U.S. and U.S.S.R.* (New York: Pocket Books, 1973): pp. 69-73.

13. Barbara B. Varenhorst, "Training Adolescents as Peer Counselors," *Personnel and Guidance Journal,* 53, 4 (December 1974): pp 271 275.

14. Robert Schreck, *et al.,* "The Metamorphosis of Lee High School," p. 208.

15. *Ibid.,* pp. 214-215.

16. John P. DeCecco and Arlene K. Richards, *Growing Pains: Uses of School Conflict,* p. 189.

17. *Ibid.,* pp. 214-215.

18. Stanley G. Sanders and Janis S. Yarbrough, "Bringing Order to an Inner-City Middle School," *Phi Delta Kappan,* 58, 4 (December 1976): pp. 333-334.

7

Developing a Team Approach to Discipline Problems

Goal Number 4: In as many cases as possible, shift responsibility for diagnosing and managing behavior problems from individuals to teams.

THE SUGGESTION THAT SERIOUS student behavior problems be handled by teams rather than individuals comes at a time when teachers feel more and more isolated. Calls are heard from professional organizations for more collaborative decision-making so that all school personnel can experience a sense of ownership in the educational enterprise. Some schools have implemented team-teaching arrangements to facilitate collegial interaction. Teams bring together individuals with different perspectives on student problems, their identification, and their treatment. Teachers who teach or plan in teams often express feelings of greater competence in dealing with the students under their supervision.

FACULTY TROUBLESHOOTING

Recommendation Number 4.1: *Anticipation of problems by troubleshooting teams.* Teachers working with the same students should form grade-level teams. These teams should convene periodically for troubleshooting — anticipating problems before they become major upsets.

The idea of troubleshooting — trying to pool perceptions in order to anticipate problems before they become serious — originally gained popularity in government and industry. The SMPSD is based on the belief that such a process also can contribute to a reduction in student behavior problems. School personnel try to alert each other to which students are beginning to have problems in order to be able to intervene more effectively. An increasing number of secondary schools appear to be adopting some form of troubleshooting.[1]

Is a troubleshooting session simply a glorified faculty meeting? Anyone who has ever endured a faculty meeting realizes that it rarely confronts the concerns of specific students. Such gatherings simply are too large and too oriented to general organizational business to be effective in handling the problems of individual students. As one insightful principal phrased it,

Today's high schools have myriads of forces that can distract administrators and teachers from concentrating on the needs of kids. These forces are often the front-burner survival issues with which the principal must deal.[2]

Teachers attending faculty meetings frequently report that the meetings are not focusing on issues that really matter to them. They also maintain that specific decisions affecting students often are not made collaboratively. One study indicated that school psychologists were perceived to make too many unilateral decisions regarding students with problems.[3] Teachers want to contribute to improvements in individual student behavior, but they lack the organizational encouragement and support to undertake such endeavors.

In order for troubleshooting not to bog down in managerial matters, a few guidelines should be considered.

> **Recommendation Number 4.1.1:** *Specificity of discussion.* Discussions must involve references to specific students rather than broad statements, vague feelings, or anecdotes.

> **Recommendation Number 4.1.2:** *Need for confidentiality.* All discussions must be kept in strictest confidence.

Recommendation Number 4.1.3: *Planning of specific actions.* For each student discussed during a troubleshooting session, a specific plan of action must be adopted before the session ends.

Recommendation Number 4.1.4: *Delegation of responsibility.* One person must assume responsibility for seeing that the plan of action is implemented. Responsibilities should be distributed equitably (i.e., counselors should not always be selected).

Recommendation Number 4.1.5: *Regular feedback on cases.* The individual responsible for seeing that the plan of action is implemented must report back to the group at the next session about its success.

Recommendation Number 4.1.6: *Documentation of proceedings.* Minutes should be taken of all troubleshooting session proceedings.

CASE CONFERENCES AND RESOURCE PEOPLE

Despite the best intentions of those who participate in troubleshooting and the most carefully structured guidelines, the early identification of problems will not always succeed in preventing the onset of major difficulties. On occasions when a plan of action generated during a troubleshooting session proves unsuccessful, a case conference should be scheduled.

Recommendation Number 4.2: *Follow-up case conferences.* Case conferences should be scheduled for any student who continues to experience problems after a plan of action has been developed at a troubleshooting session.

The case conference represents a more intensive exploration of one student's problems than is possible at a troubleshooting session. The composition of a case conference also is different. Only those teachers having direct contact with the student under discussion are invited. The student's counselor, an administrator, the school nurse, and the school psychologist are other possible resource people. In most case conferences, the student and his or her parents should be in attendance. The strict guidelines governing troubleshooting sessions probably will not be necessary at a case conference, but it may be desirable to appoint a chairperson to take notes and formulate a formal agreement at the close of the meeting. A contract signed by all parties, including the student's teachers, sometimes may be appropriate.

One advantage enjoyed by the case conference is that the student's problem is recognized before the meeting is held. Advance warning permits some preliminary fact-finding. It also allows the student's counselor to try and contact any resource people from outside the school. Including the student's minister, Scout leader, coach, pediatrician, sibling or friend in case-conference deliberations may well provide just the insight necessary to develop an effective strategy.

With regard to the involvement of outside resource people, it is unfortunate that school personnel usually are unaware of individuals on whom they can call for assistance in dealing with student problems. For this reason, school officials need to establish an inventory of potential resource people available to assist in school intervention efforts.

> **Recommendation Number 4.3:** *Inventory of potential resources.* An inventory should be made of potential resource persons who would be willing to assist in case conferences.

> **Recommendation Number 4.3.1:** *Informal resource persons' meetings.* An effort should be made to have the resource persons meet together periodically on an informal basis to discuss general concerns and school discipline policies.

A variety of individuals with useful knowledge about young people reside or work in most communities. The following list is suggestive of some of these resource persons:

Athletes
Child-welfare workers
Clergy
Coaches (nonschool athletics)
Judges
Planned Parenthood workers
Police personnel
Probation officers
Psychiatric social workers
Pediatricians
Scout leaders
Television and radio personalities
Youth-organization directors.

Bringing to case conferences expertise from the community benefits the school in general as well as the students under discussion. Resource people can be important allies when they gain an appreciation for the problems educators face on a daily basis. Including community resource persons in the team effort to reduce behavior problems also constitutes a valuable gesture of humility. In an era when too many school employees react defensively to public concern over education, such actions can be of great symbolic worth. If presented with *specific* problems to help resolve, many members of communities, despite busy schedules, will lend their assistance.

The team approach need not focus exclusively on the diagnosis of student problems or the prescription of treatments. Teams also may become involved in actual intervention efforts. W. Conrad Powell described one project in which an "intervention center" for delinquency-prone students was established with the assistance of various public agencies.[4] The center was designed to be accessible to troubled young people and to eliminate the fragmented nature of local youth services. Organized to provide group and individual counseling, the center received material and moral support from mental health and public health services, juvenile courts, the youth services bureau, and the Neighborhood Youth Corps.

Recommendation Number 4.4: *Employment of additional resource personnel.* When possible, school

> officials should locate funds to hire special resource
> people to participate on a regular basis in case con-
> ferences and other team activities.

While public-spirited volunteers are an asset to any team effort, there is no substitute for paid part-time or full-time specialists. Since more federal, state, local, and private funds have become available to schools in recent years and school discipline is currently a prime concern among the public, it may be possible for school officials to secure enough money to employ resource-persons with expertise in dealing with student behavior problems. Where universities and medical centers are close, the possibility also exists that experts-in-training can be obtained for relatively little cost. Participating in a team effort to reduce behavior problems would constitute a valuable field experience for many young teachers, psychologists, social workers, physicians, and school administrators.

Outside experts, hired or voluntary, can be used in other ways besides members of case-conference teams. A pediatrician-in-residence at a school can provide school personnel with advice on behavior problems that seem to have physiological origins.[5] There is evidence, in fact, that pediatricians are becoming more concerned about school-related problems. Data suggests that larger percentages of their private practices are being devoted to these matters.[6] Some pediatricians believe that the schools can be more effective than parents in carrying out clinical recommendations.[7] An alliance between educators and medical personnel may improve the chances of gaining the cooperation of young people possessing health problems.

Not all resource people need serve solely as consultants to schools. When New Haven's Lee High School faced growing racial tension, it hired a social worker, with the rank of assistant principal, to serve as a community coordinator.[8] Perhaps a psychologist specializing in adolescence would make a good dean of students. An off-duty policeman could be a useful addition to the guidance department. Whoever the resource person, it must be remembered, however, that to be effective the individual should be selected with the advice and consent of members of the school community.

USING HUMAN RESOURCES MORE EFFECTIVELY

Recommendation Number 4.5: *Utilization of existing staff in new roles.* New ways of utilizing existing staff more effectively in collaborative efforts to reduce behavior problems should be considered.

Sometimes it may not be possible or desirable to hire outside experts or obtain volunteers in order to supplement a team approach to improved school discipline. In such instances, it may be valuable to rethink the role descriptions of existing personnel. Too often those who work in formal organizations such as schools feel that job descriptions are etched in stone, never to be altered. There is no reason, though, why school personnel cannot meet together and decide what changes in their functions could lead to fewer student behavior problems. The Individually Guided Education program, along with a host of alternative schools, has demonstrated, for example, that teachers also make very effective student advisors — when they have sufficient time. Patricia Maslon described a program in which a counselor served as a consultant to a team of teachers.[9] In this new role, the counselor assisted actively in the planning and teaching of courses in which many of his "problem" students were enrolled. Gavriel Solomon believes school psychologists can be more effective as organizational psychologists than as clinical psychologists.[10] Their duties could include the assessment of school climate and organizational effectiveness as well as staff development designed to train teachers how to deal more productively with student behavior problems. Another role modification might be to invite members of the Board of Education to join in planning and implementing the SMPSD. Encouraging Board members to become part of this kind of team effort makes sense, first because respected community representatives often have many insights to offer and second because the awareness of daily school problems needs to be cultivated in top-level decision-makers.

Recommendation Number 4.6: *Student membership on problem-solving teams.* Students should be re-

garded as essential members of any team designed
to work on improving school discipline.

Students clearly are among the least effectively used human resources in most schools. The reasons why student involvement in the SMPSD is important are obvious, though. First, students have a *right* to provide input for planning what directly affects them. Second, student input is valuable information when matters related to their own behavior are being deliberated.[11] Third, involving students may enhance their sense of ownership in the school, thus stimulating more responsible behavior. When adults insist on unilaterally resolving all problems and planning all new activities, they encourage students to remain dependent and irresponsible.

Inviting students to participate in team discussions of behavior problems and to help develop strategies for dealing with troubled peers is a major step toward the growth of social responsibility. In fact, a large-scale study at Johns Hopkins' Center for Social Organization of Schools found that "student involvement in governing decisions and instructional choices in school has a measurable positive impact on attitudes opposing vandalism and on non-aggressive student relations with teachers."[12] Thus a fourth reason for involving students in decision-making seems to be that the process itself can lead to positive results.

Additional support for student involvement comes from behavior-modification advocates. Teachers are urged to include students in the process of modifying the behavior of disruptive peers. When inappropriate classroom behavior is reinforced by student attention, teachers might seek student assistance in ignoring the behavior until it subsides.[13] Students also can collect baseline data and aid in providing systematic reinforcement for appropriate conduct.

An elementary district in Arizona used students in a program intended to reduce unexcused absences among a group of 89 chronic absentees.[14] First, the absentees were involved in selecting the rewards they wished to receive if their attendance improved. Then, each absentee was paired with two of his or her friends who attended school regularly. The combination of material rewards (usually small toys or candy) and peer encouragement proved to be an effective strategy for reducing truancy.

In another elementary school, a fifth grader was trained as a "behavioral engineer" to improve the behavior of four first graders.[15] The first-grade students were failing to complete assignments and walking around class disturbing others. By employing a system of lights to notify these four students when they were off-task, the fifth grader produced improvements in the conduct of all four first graders.

Involving older students in school discipline also offers a variety of possibilities. Mention already has been made of the value of student participation in rule-making and conflict resolution. With another kind of approach, one high school established groups of four students, three teachers, and an outside facilitator and directed them to explore teacher-student relations in a systematic way.[16] Teachers who participated in the groups were impressed with how seriously the students took their responsibilities and with their contributions. Among other items, students commented on their teachers' lack of respect for them, the arbitrary nature of many school rules, and the archaic quality of much instruction. At the same time, the students indicated that most teachers made a sincere effort to be friendly and helpful. Out of such discussions can come considerable good will, as well as a specific agenda for school improvements.

Sometimes the student behavior problems facing a school require intensive short-term deliberation rather than protracted discussions. Conflict-resolution procedures and troubleshooting sessions are not appropriate. In addition, outside expertise may be needed. For such occasions, school officials may need to initiate special task forces consisting of school and community representatives.

Recommendation Number 4.7: *Initiation of special task forces for acute problems.* Special task forces should be used to attack acute or special problems requiring intensive, short-term collaboration, definite decisions, and a relatively high degree of local publicity.

Developing a Team Approach to Discipline Problems

Recommendations for Faculty Troubleshooting Teams:

4.1   Anticipation of problems
        by troubleshooting teams.
4.1.1   Specificity of discussion.
4.1.2   Need for confidentiality.
4.1.3   Planning of specific
        actions.
4.1.4   Delegation of responsibility.
4.1.5   Regular feedback on cases.
4.1.6   Documentation of proceedings.

Additional Recommendations:

4.2   Follow-up case
        conferences.
4.3   Inventory of potential resources.
4.3.1   Informal resource persons'
        meetings.
4.4   Employment of additional
        resource personnel.
4.5   Utilization of existing staff
        in new roles.
4.6   Student membership on
        problem-solving teams.
4.7   Initiation of special task
        forces for acute problems.

Goal Number 4: In as many cases as possible, shift responsibility for diagnosing and managing behavior problems from individuals to teams.

These kinds of problems with which a special task force can deal include school vandalism, theft, and drug use. School and community can join together to try and eliminate violence on television. Mel Gross, a principal from Cleveland, Ohio, described a "Youth Task Force" that was established at his high school to work on attendance problems.[17] Seven community agencies, a minister, and school counselors collaborated with students in an effort to help chronic truants. In a recent Gallup Poll, in fact, more people felt that special school task forces were needed to deal with discipline problems than with any other area of school concern.[18]

By creating task forces consisting of school personnel and community representatives, school officials can acknowledge publicly that problems exist while simultaneously demonstrating that something constructive is being done to correct them. Task forces may be empowered to convene special hearings during school hours so that student testimony can be gathered. Students may be "hired" by task forces as special investigators to assist in fact-finding operations. By agreeing to meet for a designated number of times, task forces also can enlist the assistance of busy outside experts more easily than can ongoing school groups.

Following their meetings, task forces may publish statements on the status of the problems under investigation and recommend policy changes to school officials.

Thus far little mention has been made of parent participation in the foregoing team efforts or other components of the SMPSD. This fact is not due to oversight. Parental input is considered *so* critical to school discipline that a separate chapter has been reserved for its discussion. The following chapter will present suggestions on how to include parents in efforts to deal with student behavior problems.

Notes

1. Daniel L. Duke, "How Administrators View the Crisis in School Discipline," *Phi Delta Kappan,* 59, 5 (January 1978): 12.
2. Gerald L. Haines, "The Management Team: Advocates for Kids, a

High School Principal's Perspective," *Thrust*, 6, 2 (November 1976): 7.

3. Irwin Hyman, *et al.*, "Patterns of Interprofessional Conflict Resolution on School Child Study Teams," *Journal of School Psychology*, 11, 3 (Fall 1973): 187-195.

4. W. Conrad Powell, "Educational Intervention As a Preventive Measure" in Ernst A. Wenk (ed.), *Delinquency Prevention and the Schools*, Sage Contemporary Social Science Issues 29 (Beverly Hills, California: Sage Publications, 1976) pp. 113-115.

5. A pediatrician-in-residence program currently is being tried in Galveston, Texas, and another is being contemplated at Stanford Medical Center.

6. Robert J. Haggerty, "The Changing Role of the Pediatrician in Child Health Care," *American Journal of Disturbed Children*, 127 (April 1974): 545-549.

7. Sydney S. Gellis (ed.), *Yearbook of Pediatrics - 1976* (Chicago: Year Book Medical Publishers, Inc., 1976), p. 339.

8. Robert Schreck, *et al.*, "The Metamorphosis of Lee High School," *Urban Education*, 10, 2 (July 1975).

9. Patricia J. Maslon, "The School Counselor As Collaborative Consultant: A Program for Counseling and Teaching in the Secondary School Classroom," *Adolescence*, 9, 33 (Spring 1974): 97-106.

10. Private Communication from Professor Gavriel Solomon, Hebrew University, Israel.

11. For a discussion of student contributions to school improvement see Daniel Duke, "What Can Students Tell Educators About Classroom Dynamics?" *Theory Into Practice*, 16, 3 (June 1977): 262-271.

12. James M. McPartland and Edward L. McDill, *The Unique Role of Schools in the Causes of Youthful Crime*, Report No. 216 (Baltimore: Center for Social Organization of Schools, 1976), p. iii.

13. For a discussion of some behavior-modification possibilities for students see N. L. Gage and David Berliner, *Educational Psychology* (Chicago: Rand McNally College Publishing Company, 1975), pp. 664-665 and Howard N. Sloane, *Classroom Management* (New York: John Wiley and Sons, Inc., 1976), pp. 130-147.

14. Ronald R. Morgan, "An Exploratory Study of Three Procedures to Encourage School Attendance," *Psychology in the Schools*, 12, 2 (April 1975): pp. 209-215.

15. Paul R. Surratt, Roger Ulrich, and Robert P. Hawkins, "An Elementary Student As a Behavioral Engineer," in Roger Ulrich, *et al.* (eds.), *Control of Human Behavior* (Glenview, Ill.: Scott, Foresman, 1970), pp. 263-270.

16. Ronald J. Fisher, "A Discussion Project on High School Adolescents' Perceptions of the Relationship between Students and Teachers," *Adolescence,* 11, 41 (Spring 1976): 87-95.

17. Mel Gross, "Community Involvement Helps Relieve Attendance Problems," *NASSP Bulletin,* 61, 408 (April 1977): 115-116.

18. George H. Gallup, "Eighth Annual Gallup Poll of the Public's Attitudes Toward the Public Schools," *Phi Delta Kappan,* 58, 2 (October 1976): 191-192.

8

Involving Parents in School Discipline

Goal Number 5: Involve parents in the diagnosis and resolution of student behavior problems as well as in prevention programs.

I N A RECENT ARTICLE on the importance of parental involvement in schools, R. Gary Bridge concluded, "The family makes a significant difference in a child's performance and eventual life chances, and any school innovation aimed at increasing individual performance should build on or redirect the resources of the family."[1] Research evidence confirms the value of parental involvement. One study, for example, found that schools where parents were actively concerned about the quality of their children's education also tended to have higher levels of student achievement.[2] *Time* reported on dramatic improvements in student achievement and behavior as a result of involving inner-city parents in their children's schooling.[3] Child Parent Education Centers, established in Chicago and funded by Title I, demonstrated that the achievement gap between students from disadvantaged and advantaged backgrounds can be narrowed considerably by developing parent-teacher-student collaboration on a continuing basis.[4] The administration of Yerba Buena High School in San Jose, California, found that students' attitudes toward school improved as a result of parental participation in conflict-resolution activities.[5] W. B. Brookover discovered that good parent-school relations enhanced the effectiveness of the school guidance program.[6]

The implication of these and other reports is that educators make a serious mistake when they regard parents as meddlesome people for whom fall "open houses" must be planned and progress notes reluctantly prepared. Bridge offered a set of six suggestions for increasing parental involvement that range from the specification of clear school statements concerning areas in which parental participation is desired or required to the use of multiple channels of home-school communications. He also cautioned against treating parents as if they were a homogeneous group all requiring similar kinds of interactions with the school.

In one study of discipline policies, over half the high school administrators indicated that parental involvement in resolving behavior problems at school was effective.[7] Fewer administrators reported involving parents in rule-making or in general decision-making related to school discipline.[8] In order for the SMPSD to function well, however, we hypothesize that parents should have opportunities to be heard at times other than when their children are in trouble.

SCHOOL-HOME COMMUNICATIONS

> **Recommendation Number 5.1:** *Parent involvement in school rule revision.* Periodically parents should be involved in reviewing and revising school rules.

> **Recommendation Number 5.2:** *Annual report to parents on discipline policies.* Parents should be notified annually of all school rules and disciplinary policies.

While it might not be possible to involve parents annually in a review of school rules, such a process should be scheduled at least every few years. During such occasions, all members of the school community can be invited to meet together and either reaffirm their satisfaction with existing policies or voice their displeasure. Following such a gathering and every fall until a new one convenes, all parents should be sent copies of the school rules and the consequences for disobeying them. Parents should have an opportunity to register any concerns they might have after reading this material. Keeping parents informed regarding school rules should increase their ability to reinforce appropriate school behavior at home.

PARENT EDUCATION

Another dimension of parental involvement is educational in nature. In the 1976 Gallup Poll of the Public's Attitudes Toward the Public Schools, over three-quarters of the people surveyed thought schools should offer courses to help parents help their children.[9] Parents even were willing to pay additional taxes to support such programs!

> **Recommendation Number 5.3:** *Provision for parent education.* The school should provide opportunities for parents to gain new skills and knowledge related to childrearing and behavior problems.

There is no reason why the educational horizons of elementary and secondary schools should be limited to children and adolescents. As the current popularity of do-it-yourself books on psychology suggests, parents desire more understanding of how they and their children function. The literature on child development has firmly established the importance of good parenting in the growth of healthy youngsters. Using some of this research as a basis for parent-education seminars might be one way that schools can help involve parents in the SMPSD. Teachers and other school employees should be urged to participate as well. While Chapter 10 deals specifically with teacher education programs, it is worth noting at this point that teachers can benefit from working with parents to achieve a greater understanding of young people.

Various formats for parent education programs are possible. Videotapes might be taken of actual classes in operation. When replayed during an informal evening seminar, the videotapes could serve as the basis for discussion and critical analysis. Parents who never have an opportunity to visit their children's classes during the day could gain an appreciation for what occurs on a routine basis.

A second possibility could involve inviting community resource people to address parents and teachers on specific topics. If such sessions are held in local homes, much of the formalized atmosphere of the school auditorium can be eliminated. Topics for presentations might include a variety of timely issues, such as the following:

1. Juvenile law and justice
2. Student rights
3. Community resources available for troubled youth
4. Parental discipline
5. Alternative learning programs
6. Drug and alcohol problems
7. Diagnosing learning problems
8. Dealing with student behavior problems during a period of fiscal cutbacks.

The Tucson Community Education Project has extended the notion of community resource development by reconceptualizing the elementary school as the hub of a community education program serving "students" of all ages. In a three-phase undertaking, the Tucson project first involved parents in strengthening the K-6 curriculum in participating schools through such activities as teaching elective courses and serving as guest speakers. The second and third phases of the project developed extensive afterschool and evening programs for community members. In the area of school discipline, parent and community volunteers assisted school personnel by taking attendance and preparing attendance records, supervising classrooms while teachers had individual or small-group conferences, and serving as counselors to solve minor concerns before they develop into discipline problems. Such a reconceptualization of the school as the center of community education programs facilitates parent involvement in school activities.

The suggestions so far apply to parents in general. Some parent-education programs, however, might be designed for specific groups — such as the parents of students specifically experiencing discipline problems. Educators who have tried to initiate such programs indicate that they are well received. Though initially embarrassed by being identified publicly as the parents of "problem children," those attending after-school meetings express relief when they discover that others have similar concerns. Informal gatherings devoted to the open discussion of childrearing problems can provide parents with the much-needed group support they have failed to receive because of their reluctance to share their problems.

Don Dinkmeyer presented one type of problem-oriented activity called the Parent "C" Group.[10] Designed to enable members to acquire knowledge and to evaluate their own beliefs, the "C" Group consists of from five to eight parents and a leader skilled in group dynamics. The group begins with parents discussing some of their concerns regarding their children. Parents are asked to identify a specific behavioral incident and to share their feelings when their children misbehaved. The leader is careful to encourage parents to be supportive of each other while exploring possible solutions to child-related problems. The underlying assumption of the "C" Group is that parents can change a child's behavior only if they are willing to alter their own behavior first.

Variations on the Parent "C" Group theme are offered by followers of Thomas Gordon (Parent Effectiveness Training) and Rudolf Dreikurs. Additional programs to help parents deal with their children derive from the work of William Glasser (Parent-Involvement Program) and behavior-modification specialists. A concise review of some of these programs has been provided by Catherine Brown.[11] Her critical analysis of Gordon, Dreikurs, Glasser, and behavior-modification advocates is valuable for anyone considering the development of school-based parent education programs.

Others have been active in parent education. Counselors at Berkeley's East Campus Continuation School established a family-counseling service for the school's most troubled students.[12] Intensive group and individual family-counseling are available for no charge to help families regain a productive sense of trust and unity. Erhard Seminars Training (est) operates training programs for both parents and their children. Part of the focus of this training concerns making and keeping agreements.

The ultimate value of schools that serve as centers for parent education derives from the new relationships that can grow between parents and educators. Parents have the opportunity to discover how much teachers care about young people. Teachers see that parents share many of their own anxieties and uncertainties. Parent-education programs can be useful springboards to parent-teacher alliances. Such alliances are essential in an era when no single group has the power to achieve reforms in schools.

KEEPING PARENTS POSTED

Another way — though one less pleasant in many instances than parent education — that educators can demonstrate that they care about parents as well as students is by keeping parents informed about their children's progress in school. Such a suggestion probably sounds too obvious to mention. After all, most schools print thousands of "progress reports" (a strange label considering the usual content of these forms) for use by teachers and counselors. Unfortunately, parents tend to be notified only when serious problems have developed with their children. The possibility of effective parental intervention at such times is greatly reduced. School personnel should routinely inform parents of any signs of problems in their children's work or behavior. Naturally, indications of improved work and behavior also should be noted.

> **Recommendation Number 5.4:** *Immediate parent notification of problems.* Parents should be informed of problems involving their children as soon as possible. Direct contact or contact over the telephone is preferable to written notification. When the latter course of action must be followed, letters should be mailed special delivery (return receipt requested) or entrusted to a courier.

> **Recommendation Number 5.4.1:** *Verification of student absences.* Parents should be contacted on a routine basis to verify absences.

> **Recommendation Number 5.4.2:** *Daily telephoning hour.* An hour each day should be set aside for tele-

phone calls to parents whose children are beginning to experience problems in school. Responsibility for the home telephoning can be shared among administrators, counselors, and perhaps a trusted executive secretary.

Experienced educators feel that effective school-home communications depend on the development of a daily routine. Teachers, administrators, and counselors should *expect* to spend a portion of each day on the telephone with parents. The time need be no more than ten minutes, set aside specifically for telephoning good or bad news. Calls can be made to students as well as parents. For example, students can be informed of assignments when they are absent, problems that might be difficult to handle face-to-face can be discussed, or wishes for a speedy recovery from an illness can be extended. If time for such calls is not set aside, however, it is likely that the press of daily chores will prevent regular school-home contacts.

In addition to maintaining telephone contact with homes, some schools have established community-liaison offices.[13] Liaisons typically are people from local neighborhoods hired to keep in touch with community concerns and to assist in parental contact and conflict resolution. Liaisons can be particularly useful in dealing with the problems of minority families, many of which are distrustful of school authorities. When students must be sent home because of behavior problems, liaisons can serve as escorts as well as people who can explain the exact nature of the problems to concerned parents.

PARENTS AND CONFLICT-RESOLUTION

An additional way in which parents can be involved in the SMPSD concerns the resolution of school-related problems involving their children. In the previous chapter, mention was made of case conferences to which parents should be invited. Even if problems are not serious enough to warrant case conferences though, it may be important to obtain parental input and approval.

Recommendation Number 5.5: *Parent involvement in problem resolution.* Parents should be involved in resolving major discipline problems involving their children.

Some behavior problems obviously are so minor that parental involvement is not necessitated. When, however, problems occur so frequently or are so serious that a student's progress in school is threatened, parents should participate in resolution efforts. Holding a pre-suspension hearing is one occasion when parents can join school officials and the accused student to attempt to reach agreement on how to prevent the reoccurrence of problem behavior. Parents may be asked to sign a "contract" in which they consent to supervise a particular course-of-action designed to reduce misconduct by their children. In a recent Gallup Poll, in fact, a majority of respondents even agreed that parents whose children are frequently absent from school should be brought to court and fined![14]

While court action may not be the best way to ensure it, parental involvement and support are critical to the overall effectiveness of the SMPSD. Too often, it seems, educators spend more time trying to lay the blame for poor student behavior at parents' doorsteps than extending opportunities to parents to assist in improving student performance. Most parents — even those with "problem" children — care deeply about their offspring. What teachers and administrators interpret as parental disinterest or hostility often may simply be uneasiness around school authorities or distrust of large organizations. On some occasions parents neglect to become more involved in their children's education simply because they are unaware of the possibilities open to them. It is up to school personnel to inform parents of their options as well as to make them feel wanted when they come to discuss their children.

In a fascinating story of one high school's efforts to involve parents in school decision-making, Susan Jacoby related the fact that parents did not realize they were able to attend school governance meetings.[15] As a result, rumors and feelings of powerlessness spread. Only a concerted push by the principal and his staff convinced parents that the school was theirs too. Better public relations at an earlier time would have spared this particular school a trying period just prior to school board elections.

School personnel also should be aware that developing an active parent-involvement component requires a good deal of administrative energy, initial time commitment, and organizational support. Don Davies makes the point in *Schools Where Parents Make a Difference* that the essential difference between schools with and schools without successful parent programs is that the successful schools alter the school structure to accommodate parents — whether it be a permanent parent council or an ongoing reward system for parent participation. Davies also notes that exemplary parent programs provide some training in decision-making and planning skills for parents. In addition, he recommends that schools hire paid staff members to develop and maintain parent organizations.[16]

Recommendations: Involving Parents in School Discipline

5.1   Parent involvement in
        school rule-revision.

5.2   Annual report to parents
        on discipline policies.

5.3   Provision for parent
        education.

5.4   Immediate parent notification
        of problems.

5.4.1   Verification of student
        absences.

5.4.2   Daily telephoning hour.

5.5   Parent involvement in
        problem resolution.

Goal Number 5: Involve parents in the diagnosis and resolution of student behavior problems as well as in prevention programs.

An ongoing parent council could assist in many of the previously described activities related to the development of the SMPSD.[17] Some of these are:

1. Assessing student, faculty, and community needs and perceptions regarding student discipline (data collection)
2. Selecting resource personnel for troubleshooting teams
3. Assisting in publicizing school rules and communicating school problems to the community.

Whether parents choose to become actively involved in the SMPSD is not within the power of school personnel to determine. The latter must make certain, though, that every parent has an opportunity to participate and that when they participate, they are supported and rewarded for their investment of time and energy.

Notes

1. R. Gary Bridge, "Parent Participation in School Innovations," *Teachers College Record,* 77, 3 (February 1976): 366-384.
2. William G. Spady, "The Impact of School Resources on Students" in Fred N. Kerlinger (ed.), *Review of Research in Education,* 1 (Itasca, Illinois: F. E. Peacock Publishers, Inc., 1973), p. 168.
3. *Time* (November 8, 1976), 77.
4. A. Jackson Stenner and Siegried G. Mueller, "A Successful Compensatory Education Model," *Phi Delta Kappan,* 55, 4 (December 1973): 246-248.
5. John Sellarole and Jerry Mullins, "Management in a Team Structure" in Ruth Pritchard and Virginia Wedra (eds.), *A Resource Manual for Reducing Conflict in California Schools* (Sacramento: California School Boards Association, 1975), pp. 20-21.
6. W. B. Brookover, "Self-concept of Ability and School Achievement in H. L. Miller (ed.), *Education for the Disadvantaged* (New York: The Free Press, 1967).
7. Daniel L. Duke, "How Administrators View the Crisis in School Discipline" *Phi Delta Kappan,* 59, 5 (January 1978).
8. *Ibid.,* 11.

9. George H. Gallup, "Eighth Annual Gallup Poll of the Public's Attitudes Toward the Public Schools," *Phi Delta Kappan,* 58, 2 (October 1976): 193.

10. Don C. Dinkmeyer, "The Parent 'C' Group," *Personnel and Guidance Journal,* 52, 4 (December 1973): 252-256.

11. Catherine Caldwell Brown, "It Changed My Life," *Psychology Today,* 10 (November 1976): 47-57.

12. Jerald Kramer, "The East Campus Family Counseling Program," *Phi Delta Kappan,* 57, 6 (February 1976): 417.

13. Jerry Mullins, "The Interagency Team Concept" in Ruth Pritchard and Virginia Wedra (eds.), *A Resource Manual for Reducing Conflict and Violence in California Schools* (Sacramento: California School Boards Association, 1975), pp. 13-14.

14. George H. Gallup, "Ninth Annual Gallup Poll of the Public's Attitudes Toward the Public Schools," *Phi Delta Kappan,* 59, 1 (September 1977): 37-38.

15. Susan Jacoby, "What Happened When a High School Tried Self-Government," *Saturday Review* (April 1, 1972): 49-53.

16. Don Davies, *Schools Where Parents Make a Difference.* (Boston: Institute for Responsive Education, 1976).

17. An excellent manual, originally developed for School Site Councils in California but applicable to any parent-teacher-student collaborative effort, is Jean Rosaler's "How to Make the Best School Site Council in the World" (California State Board of Education, 1979). Rosaler details how to involve parents in school councils, how to keep them interested, what skills to teach them, and what pitfalls to avoid in coping with the needs of parents, teachers, and students.

9

Providing Reinforcing Environments for Learning

Goal Number 6: Rather than trying to curtail behavior problems simply by increasing punishments, reinforce regularly those student behaviors that contribute to a healthy school environment.

THE GOAL OF THE sixth component of the SMPSD echoes a theme present in most behavior-modification literature — to obtain desirable behavior, reinforce desirable behavior. Punishing students when they exhibit undesirable behavior will not ensure that they will know how to act appropriately in the future. All too often adults are quick to criticize and punish youngsters for problem behavior, while neglecting to praise them for routine acts of politeness and consideration. Good behavior should not be taken for granted.

PRIVILEGES

Unfortunately, educators along with other adults frequently do take good behavior for granted. At the same time, young people who misbehave are offered rewards to get them "back on the right track." For instance, a chronically truant student will be given the privilege of leaving school early if he attends morning class on a regular basis. A "difficult" girl will be permitted to work as an office aide if she stops insulting her teachers. Such rewards are viewed as instruments of social control and may be essential for improved behavior, but they convey a confusing message to those who behave appropriately most of the time. Why should the latter group continue to obey school rules when their less law-abiding peers disobey the rules and receive rewards for acting better?

The SMPSD provides privileges for students who regularly obey school rules. Students themselves should be involved in determining these privileges.

> **Recommendation Number 6.1:** *Privileges for positive behavior.* Students who regularly obey school rules should receive certain privileges not accorded students who do not obey rules.

> **Recommendation Number 6.2:** *Student participation in the determination of rewards and sanctions.* Students should be involved in determining the privileges for good behavior as well as the consequences for disobeying rules.

The range of possible privileges for students who consistently obey rules is great. Older students seem to prefer free time or off-campus privileges. Access during free periods to the gymnasium, media center, or perhaps a special student lounge is usually valued. In determining how privileges are allocated, educators should remember to consider student behavior, not student academic achievement. Linking privileges to academic performance can unfairly penalize less able students and result in their increased frustration and demoralization. Eventually these negative feelings may themselves lead to serious discipline problems. Thus, great care should be exercised before implemneting a rewards system.

SANCTIONS

To help educators think about how to use rewards most effectively, the following matrix may be useful.

	Rewards	Sanctions
Benefits	1	2
Costs	3	4

The horizontal dimension encompasses rewards and sanctions — the two basic mechanisms by which educators obtain the behavior necessary for the accomplishment of school objectives. Benefits and costs are terms describing how rewards and sanctions are perceived by those subject to them — in this case, students.

To maximize the effectiveness of the school control structure, rewards should be perceived as beneficial (1) and sanctions as costly (4). Too frequently, however, such is not the case. Thus, a typical school sanction for truancy — suspension — is perceived by many truants as a benefit (2)! In other words, school officials actually are rewarding the truant by sending him home. In addition, school rewards sometimes are perceived by students as more costly then beneficial. For example, a trusted student may be given a position as a preceptor to help monitor the behavior of his peers. Such a role, though, may cost the student the friendship of his peers as well as time he might devote to other, more enjoyable activities.

The message is clear — the development of a system of rewards and sanctions requires a great deal of thought, planning, and student input. Sanctions, in particular, require careful consideration, since great harm can be done if they appear arbitrary, unrelated to the offense for which they are prescribed, or unduly harsh.

Several specialists have written on the subject of sanctions. Rudolf Dreikurs drew upon psychoanalytic theory to argue the merits of "logical consequences." Contrasting his approach to the traditional punishment orientation, Dreikurs and co-author Loren Grey observed:

1. Logical consequences express the reality of the social order, not of the person; punishment, the power of personal authority.
2. The logical consequence is logically related to the misbehavior; punishment rarely is.
3. Logical consequence involves no element of moral judgment; punishment inevitably does.
4. Logical consequences are concerned only with what will happen now, punishments with the past.
5. The voice is friendly when consequences are invoked; there is anger in punishment, either open or concealed.[1]

Most educators probably can cite several examples of consequences that are not logical: for instance, the low-ability student who is given an extra homework assignment because he failed to complete his classwork. Such sanctions not only lack a logical rationale; they actually may be harmful. Student respect for the school as a rule-governed organization can be undermined. In addition, certain illogical consequences actually may be criminogenic. In other wrods, they may lead to further behavior problems. This phenomenon is illustrated by the case of a troubled student who cuts class frequently. Requiring the student to attend after-school detention hall without first trying to understand his problem simply may be providing him with the opportunity to disobey another rule. If the student really is looking for attention, he learns that avoiding assigned activities is a sure way to be recognized. Rather than giving this student another chance to disobey by assigning him to detention hall, school personnel should discuss the problem with the student and negotiate consequences that contribute to improved attendance. Whatever action is taken, the earlier the intervention, the better. Attendance problems that are permitted to continue for weeks or months before action is taken are less likely to be resolved easily.

Harvey Clarizio and George McCoy, adopting a behavioral approach to dealing with behavior disorders in children, offer the following "guidelines toward a more effective use of punishment:"

1. Punishment should be used to correct behavior, not to retaliate for wrongdoing.
2. Punishment should be inherent in the situation rather than an expression of the power of one person over another. The child should experience the unpleasant but natural or logical result of his own actions.
3. The role of the teacher is to be that of a friendly bystander who is interested and objective. The teacher should avoid communicating negative feelings about the child as a person.
4. On those occasions when it is necessary for one person to punish another person, it should be done in an impersonal, matter-of-fact way. Yelling, scolding, or other vengeful accompaniment to punishment should be avoided.
5. Once a good rule has been agreed upon, there should be no

escape from its consequences. Excuses and promises should not be accepted.

6. A youngster should be given a warning or signal before punishment is delivered.

7. The nature of the punishment and the manner of presenting it should avoid the arousal of strong emotional responses in the person punished.

8. The teacher must be consistent in his use of punishment.

9. When used contingently and immediately, mild punishment can produce enduring positive change in cases where severe punishment alone fails.

10. Avoid extended periods of punishment, especially where low-intensity punishments are used.

11. Punishing inappropriate behavior is only half the story. Teachers also must reward appropriate behavior.

12. Timing plays an important role in determining the effectiveness of punishment. Children who are punished early in a given sequence of misbehavior develop greater resistance to temptation than those who are punished only after completion of the misdeed.

13. Be certain that the delivery of punishment is not associated with the giving of reinforcement. For example, if removal from the group is a rewarding experience, then it will not be effective in modifying the target behavior.

14. Punishments should be used in a way that fosters self-direction. The use of behavior contracts can be helpful.

15. It is important that the use of punishment require little of the teacher's time and energy. If delivery of the punishment is punishing to the teacher, he is apt to stop it because he is inconvenienced by the punishment rather than because the misbehavior has improved.[2]

These suggestions should be of benefit to teachers planning to implement the SMPSD in their classrooms and to school officials charged with overseeing discipline. No single approach to rewards and sanctions, though, has been found to be universally effective. Borrowing from different schools-of-thought — behavior modification, the Dreikurs' method and others — may be the only answer, as long as agreement can be reached to implement the various borrowings consistently. Still, educators should expect to be torn constantly between the desire to treat each student as an individual and the organizational pressure to handle all students the same.

Nowhere is this tension more apparent than in the realm of school discipline. For instance, opting for a Dreikurs "logical consequences" strategy may necessitate treating students differently. A logical consequence (or sanction) for one student may actually be a reward for another. To add further to the confusion, those who advocate logical consequences urge teachers to be *consistent* in applying the consequences. It may be impossible to achieve consistency while simultaneously making certain that consequences are not rewarding for certain students.

One of the perplexing realities of schooling is that every parent wants his or her child to be treated as an individual until he learns that the child has been punished while another child has not. Then the parent demands that all students be treated identically!

The best way to minimize the likelihood of conflicting disciplinary strategies probably is to involve as many members of the school community as possible in determining school rules and the consequences for disobeying them. In addition, providing periodic opportunities to evaluate the effectiveness of specific consequences will help guard against problems arising out of changing circumstances, personnel, or philosophies of discipline.

One of the most crucial guidelines listed by Clarizio and McCoy concerns the need to reward appropriate behavior. As the opening section of this chapter suggested, educators (and parents) too often take good behavior for granted. As a result, they only address themselves to youthful conduct when it is inappropriate and a reprimand or sanction is required. This approach ensures that a large number of adult-child interactions will be negative in nature.

ALTERNATIVES FOR CERTAIN STUDENTS

In some cases, the conventional public school may be unable to provide a sufficiently reinforcing environment to maximize the potential for positive student behavior. Certain students may require closer supervision, smaller classes, and more personalized instruction. These individuals seem to have difficulty adjusting on a daily basis to six different teachers and six different sets of behavior expectations (in the typical high school setting).

For these students, it may be important to create more intimate learning environments. Such environments can be found in many contemporary alternative schools.

When representatives of local school boards recently were asked to recommend programs they believed would contribute to delinquency prevention, almost 20 percent (more responses than for any other category except one) indicated "alternative schools."[3] The forementioned study by Duke and Perry discovered, in fact, that school discipline was rarely a concern in California alternative high schools. Additional support for the utilization of alternative schools to combat student behavior problems comes from a national study of disruption in urban secondary schools. The finding is clear — larger schools experience a proportionately greater number of problems.[4] The blue-ribbon National Panel on High School and Adolescent Education urged that "small, flexible, short-term, part-time schools be established and made available to all who are qualified and interested."[5]

One of the most inspiring and successful alternative schools known to the authors is Downtown Senior High in San Francisco. Each year since the late 1960s this school has provided a no-nonsense, responsive learning environment for about 250 teenagers with difficult problems — court-referred youth, dropouts, students who have failed every high school course they have taken. Almost every student graduates and secures a job. Several enroll in college. There has not been a suspension in years.

No single reason explains Downtown Senior High's success. The key lies with a collection of factors, including the following:

1. A dedicated, experienced faculty, each of whom has a counselor's credential and functions as a student advisor.
2. A tough-minded, caring principal who protects the faculty and students from red tape and who is prepared to exercise leadership when necessary.
3. Specially-designed classrooms which include private confer-

ence rooms where teachers can meet with troubled students while class is in session.

4. A work-study program which serves as a reward for students who demonstrate they can come to school regularly and behave in an adultlike way.

5. Immediate graduation upon acquisition of sufficient credits (thus students do not have to wait until June to graduate).

6. No cafeteria (students have "coffee breaks" and lunch in city restaurants).

7. Job-oriented curriculum.

In addition to the factors listed above, Downtown Senior High has on-site budgeting. Thus, the principal receives a sum of money based on the school's average enrollment and is free to allocate funds as he sees fit. Each year Emil Anderson, the principal, goes to his faculty and students and gives them the choice of how to disburse the money. They can hire security guards and deans of students or purchase electronic surveillance equipment if they wish. Or they can use the funds to hire as many teachers as possible, thus lowering the teacher-student ratio and encouraging greater personalization of instruction. Year after year, members of the school community opt for the latter.

Alternative learning environments may not all resemble Downtown Senior High. They can assume a variety of forms, including schools-within-schools, schools-without-walls, work-study programs, and learning centers. Individually Guided Education (IGE), a packaged program designed to foster comprehensive school improvement, calls for the reorganization of participating schools into smaller, more personalized learning communities, each with approximately ten teachers and 250 students. Some large secondary schools are adopting house systems in order to give students a sense of identity with a particular group of teachers and students. In settings with fewer students, it is easier for educators to reinforce appropriate behavior and counsel students who experience difficulties.

Recommendation Number 6.3: *Provision for alternative learning environments.* Schools should provide optional learning environments for students needing more personalized attention and less rigid behavior expectations.

Alternative schools and other optional programs may not always be appropriate for students with problems or special needs. Some may require short-term intervention designed to allow them to continue their regular studies while simultaneously focusing on their problems. These kinds of programs resemble the workshops given to people with speeding violations in lieu of a fine or license revocation.

Many schools have instituted "in-school suspension" programs to accommodate truants who view a five-day suspension as a welcome vacation from school.[6] Under this arrangement, suspended students must come to school and work all day on regular assignments under the supervision of a special person. Variations on this approach include "Saturday school," after-school programs, and crisis-intervention centers.[7] Sometimes these programs provide for direct instruction in adolescent psychology, values-clarification, and interpersonal relations. Students analyze why they cannot function well in a regular school setting. These programs typically are staffed by teachers with special training in group dynamics, abnormal psychology, and conflict management.

On occasion neither an alternative school nor a short-term, in-school program seems adequate for troubled youngsters. These individuals may be referred to an intensive out-of-school program such as Outward Bound. Such challenging adventure-oriented experiences can "reach" many students who are thought to be beyond help.[8]

California has created a different kind of alternative. Project Furlough is directed at students "who are recognized by their teachers, counselors, or parents as just barely hanging on so far as attendance in high school is concerned."[9] Instead of letting these students drop out of school entirely, Project Furlough permits school officials to assign them to special counselors. Counselors help locate employment for the students and evaluate their performance for graduation purposes. Students do not have to attend classes, but must check in with their counselor once a week.

Recommendation Number 6.4: *Provision for short-term behavior improvement programs.* Schools should provide short-term programs focusing on behavior improvement for students temporarily unable or unwilling to conform to school rules.

PEER-GROUP INFLUENCE

While educators must strive to make regular schools and optional programs as reinforcing of positive behavior as possible, they cannot do the job alone. Since the adolescent peer group is one of the most powerful influences on teenage behavior, we deem it prudent to try and develop the peer group as a force working toward positive outcomes. Too often, teachers and parents seem to assume that the peer group is preordained to challenge adult rules and authority. Bronfenbrenner's observations of Soviet schools suggested that the peer group also can reinforce proper standards of conduct. Research involving Mexican-American students with records of excessive unexcused absences from school indicated that peer-based reinforcement can be an effective mechanism for improving attendance behavior.[10]

Recommendation Number 6.5: *Development of positive peer-group influence.* School officials should work with students, particularly student leaders, to develop the peer group as a force acting to reinforce positive behavior.

It is never too early to encourage students to reinforce each other's appropriate behavior. One study conducted in a Virginia Infant Development Project found that aggressive behavior declined and good feelings increased among a group of kindergartners who were given a chance each day in class to tell each other about their friendly behavior.[11] By making friendliness the criterion for recognition, teachers reduced the number of bullies and cut the median number of aggressive acts per day from 42 to 9.

When a student in class behaves inappropriately in order to gain the attention or praise of peers, teachers should consider bringing the matter before the entire group. Gage and Berliner have recommended, for instance, that the teacher ask the class to join in ignoring the disruptive behavior.[12] Students also can contribute to setting the tone for good behavior by helping to develop sensible rules for their own conduct and consequences for disobedience.

In order to stimulate older students to reinforce each other for constructive conduct, school personnel may have to work more directly with student leaders than would be necessary in elementary school. Leaders include gang leaders and team captains as well as National Honor Society members and student government officials. Special workshops focusing on group dynamics and the proper exercise of leadership should be scheduled for these individuals.

CORPORAL PUNISHMENT

Nothing has been said thus far about the use of corporal punishment. Despite a recent Supreme Court decision upholding the right of school authorities to use corporal punishment, a number of experts contend that physical force does little good.[13] At worst, it actually teaches students that physical force is a legitimate way to resolve problems! An interesting finding from DeCecco and Richards' studies of conflict-resolution procedures in high schools was that school authorities actually employed physical force to settle a larger percentage of conflicts than did students.[14] Thomas Gordon, creator of Teacher Effectiveness Training, points out that "problem students" do not need more severe external controls — they need better internal controls.[15] Punishment does little to encourage the development of self-discipline.

> **Recommendation Number 6.6:** *Avoidance of corporal punishment.* Teachers and administrators should avoid the use of physical punishment to correct student behavior.

So great has the concern over corporal punishment grown that organizations dedicated to its elimination are appearing in greater numbers. One such group, End Violence Against the Next Generation, Inc., has published a pamphlet stating the reasons why it opposes corporal punishment in schools:

1. It is unnecessary.
2. It pre-empts better means of communicating with the child.
3. It teaches by example that the infliction of pain is the proper way to power.
4. It develops deviousness, the trick is not to get caught.
5. It is dangerous in that it escalates into battering.
6. It increases aggressiveness in the child and vandalism in the school.
7. It reduces the ability to concentrate on intellectual tasks.
8. It can cause sexual aberrations.
9. It causes anxiety and school phobia in the other children.
10. It damages the punisher in that it narrows his options, tunnels his vision and tarnishes his image as a man of learning.
11. It is inconsistent with any view of the child as a person worthy of respect.[16]

NO REWARDS?

Before closing this chapter, we should make mention of the possibility of eliminating the use of rewards and punishments altogether. While the nature of regular public schools may not justify comparisons with smaller, less formalized alternative schools, it is interesting to note that in the Duke and Perry study, few instances were found where students were systematically rewarded for appropriate behavior or punished for misconduct.[17] Despite this fact, behavior problems were minimal. Students were encouraged *and expected* to behave well because they had *chosen* to attend the alternative school. Students enjoyed having a voice in determining how the school would be run. Students in these schools realized that unconstructive behavior would mean transfer back to their former schools or denial of credit toward graduation. Such consequences generally were accepted as reasonable alternatives to conventional punishments.

The alternative school study illustrated how some schools, particularly small ones, can function without elaborate sets of rules and sanctions. In those situations where a relatively large number of rules may be required, care should be taken to involve students in the development of rules, sanctions, and rewards.

Providing Reinforcing Environments for Learning

Recommendations:

6.1   Privileges for positive behavior.

6.2   Student participation in the determination of rewards and sanctions.

6.3   Provision for alternative learning environments.

6.4   Provision for short-term behavior improvement programs.

6.5   Development of positive peer-group influence.

6.6   Avoidance of corporal punishment.

Goal Number 6: Rather than trying to curtail behavior problems simply by increasing punishments, reinforce regularly those student behaviors that contribute to a healthy school environment.

Notes

1. Rudolf Dreikurs and Loren Gray, *A New Approach to Discipline: Logical Consequences* (New York: Hawthorn Books, Inc., 1968), pp. 71-78.

2. Harvey F. Clarizio and George F. McCoy, *Behavior Disorders in Children,* Second Edition (New York: Thomas Y. Crowell Company, 1976), pp. 509-511.

3. Richard D. Knudten, "Delinquency Programs in Schools: A Survey"

in Ernst A. Wenk (ed.), *Delinquency Prevention and the Schools,* SAGE Contemporary Social Science Issues 29 (Beverly Hills, Calif.: SAGE Publications, 1976), pp. 56-57.

4. Syracuse University Research Corporation, *Disruption in Urban Secondary Schools* (Washington, D.C.: National Association of Secondary School Principals, n.d.).

5. U. S. Department of Health, Education and Welfare, *The Education of Adolescents,* The Final Report and Recommendations of the National Panel on High School and Adolescent Education (Washington, D.C: U.S. Government Printing Office, 1976) p. 12.

6. Donald L. Harvey and William G. Moosha, "In-School Suspension: Does it Work?" *NASSP Bulletin,* 61, 405 (January 1977): 14-17.

7. For a description of one such program, see Gary J. Faltico, "An After-school School Without Failure: A New Therapy Model for Juvenile Probationers," *Corrective and Social Psychiatry,* 21, 4 (1975): 17-20.

8. For an interesting description and evaluation of the Colorado Outward Bound Program see Mary Lee Smith, *et al.,* "Evaluation of the Effects of Outward Bound" in Gene V. Glass (ed.), *Evaluation Studies Review Annual,* Volume 1, 1976 (Beverly Hills, Calif.: SAGE Publications, 1976), pp. 400-424.

9. William L. Lucas, "Experiences in a Large City School System" in James M. McPartland and Edward L. McDill (eds.), *Violence in Schools* (Lexington, Mass.: Lexington Books, 1977), pp. 74-75.

10. Ronald R. Morgan, "An Exploratory Study of Three Procedures to Encourage School Attendance," *Psychology in the Schools,* 12, 2 (April 1975): 209-215.

11. "Friendly Persuasion," *Human Behavior,* 6, 9 (September 1977): 35.

12. N. L. Gage and David Berliner, *Educational Psychology* (Chicago: Rand McNally College Publishing Company, 1975), p. 665.

13. A brief review of the Baker v. Owen decision can be found in *Phi Delta Kappan,* 57, 4 (December 1975): 288-289.

14. John P. DeCecco and Arlene K. Richards, *Growing Pains: Uses of School Conflict* (New York: Aberdeen Press, 1974), p. 115.

15. Thomas Gordon, *T.E.T.: Teacher Effectiveness Training,* (New York: Peter H. Wyden, Publisher, 1974), p. 215.

16. For research supporting these contentions, see Adam Maurer, "Corporal Punishment," *American Psychologist,* 29, 8 (August 1974): 614-626.

17. Daniel L. Duke and Cheryl Perry, "Can Alternative Schools Succeed When Benjamin Spock, Spiro Agnew, and B. F. Skinner Have Failed?" *Adolescence,* 13, 51 (Fall 1978): 375-392.

Providing Professional Development Opportunities for Faculty and Staff

Goal Number 7: Create opportunities for faculty and staff to assess local discipline problems and acquire the skills necessary for managing or reducing them.

THE SMPSD WOULD BE incomplete without provisions for the continuing professional development of school personnel. A variety of formats and foci for inservice activities exist. We will discuss several of the more promising possibilities in this chapter. It is likely, however, that the most productive activities for any faculty and staff will be those that are developed on-site through the efforts of the individuals requiring the professional development in the first place.

PLANNING PROFESSIONAL DEVELOPMENT

Recommendation Number 7.1 *Annual assessment of discipline rules and procedures.* Part of spring wrap-up activities should involve assessing the effectiveness of school rules and disciplinary procedures during the year just completed and agreeing on guidelines for the coming year.

Recommendation Number 7.1.1 *Assessment focuses planning of staff inservice.* For areas where problems are found to exist, plans should be made for appropriate inservice activities during the coming school year.

135

Many schools are allocated several days each fall prior to the commencement of classes when teachers have an opportunity for limited inservice work. Typically these preliminary gatherings are used by school officials to communicate new policies and expectations, to introduce recent additions to the faculty, and inform teachers of their assignments. On occasion, speakers may be hired to deliver inspirational addresses. Time usually is set aside for individual and departmental planning, room arrangement, and distribution of materials.

Fall planning sessions represent an excellent opportunity for working on particular elements of the SMPSD. Since memories of school discipline problems fade over the summer, efforts should be made in the spring, before school personnel disband, to lay the groundwork for fall planning. For instance, using an afternoon during the last week of school prior to summer vacation to review student behavior problems during the past year can create an excellent @starting place for fall activities. Questions can be asked concerning which school rules were useful and which consequences were not. Data collected during the year (see Chapter 5) can be presented to determine whether or not discipline-related school objectives were achieved. Student representatives can be invited to share their perceptions of behavior problems and school policies.

Equipped with notes from this spring "post mortem," school personnel can dive directly into substantive issues in the fall and avoid wasting precious planning-time trying to recall what happened the previous year. An important focus for fall activities should be specifying the skills and knowledge school personnel feel they need in order to deal effectively with student behavior problems. Once, school officials dictated what teachers required to improve themselves. In recent years, however, teachers have begun to play a more central role in determining their own inservice needs. They have moved away from workshops offered by visiting consultants and university extension courses and toward ongoing, team-oriented inservice activities locally designed to attack local problems.[1]

One of the most pressing contemporary concerns for teachers is how to acquire the special skills necessary to deal with behavior disorders in the classroom. For years new teachers have expressed the need for these skills, but more experienced teachers recently have been heard asking for additional training. If it is any comfort to American educators, Ronald Lien reported that teachers in the Soviet Union also are concerned about classroom control.[2]

In a recent review of research, Thomas Coates and Carl Thoresen indicated that student behavior problems are a primary cause of teacher anxiety. Interestingly, the reviewers noted that teacher anxiety may *cause* as well as result from student misconduct![3]

Pressure is on teacher educators to devote more attention to preparing teachers in areas of classroom management and not to dwell exclusively on subject matter. As early as 1938, though, teacher educators were being called on to provide their students with specific skills for handling classroom behavior problems.[4] Currently, the Teacher Corps, one of the most powerful forces working for educational improvement in the United States, requires each of its funded projects to provide special teacher training in behavior problems and how to deal with them. The University of Houston has an exemplary competency-based classroom management training program. The Instructional Leadership Program at Stanford University has as one of its objectives the training of experienced teachers to assume leadership for local staff development in school discipline. It is still rare, though, to find courses in schools of education that are devoted specifically to student behavior problems and school discipline.

> **Recommendation Number 7.2** *Schools of education should offer relevant coursework.* Pressure should be exerted on schools of education to offer more courses devoted to student behavior problems and school discipline.

INSERVICE PROGRAMS

Since this set of recommendations focuses on what can be done in the schools themselves to reduce behavior problems, we shall not present a detailed discussion of how schools of education can address the subject on a preservice basis. Instead, attention will be directed to professional development activities for experienced teachers.

> **Recommendation Number 7.3** *Collaborative development of inservice activities.* Inservice activities concerning how to deal effectively with student behavior problems should be undertaken collaboratively by school administrators and teachers.

While a comprehensive list of inservice activities related to student behavior has yet to be fully developed, we shall attempt in this section to present on overview of some possibilities. These include:

1. General awareness of student behavior
2. Classroom management skills
3. Interpersonal skills
4. Conflict-resolution activities
5. Academic intervention/early-warning systems.

General Awareness

Often the first (and unfortunately sometimes the only!) step in inservice activity involves making teachers *aware* of a particular problem. Awareness might center around what it means to be a student or what occurs among students while instruction supposedly is taking place. Awareness-oriented professional development is premised on the belief that teachers cannot monitor everything going on in their classes.

Various techniques have been developed to assist teachers in monitoring classroom activities. Sometimes looking at videotapes or reading an outside observer's account can provide fresh insights concerning classroom life. In one study of a dozen high school teachers, Robert Wegmann used videotape to capture the process of "maintaining discipline." Among the teacher behaviors that seemed to be critical to the process were "the judicious use of humor, good judgment in deciding whether to address an individual or a group, and facility in the redefinition of apparent challenges before they became blatant."[5]

A variety of data-collection instruments are available to assist teachers in becoming more aware of what goes on in class as they pursue their instructional objectives.[6]

Elsewhere we have urged educators to solicit student impressions of classroom life to supplement data gained from other sources.[7] Teachers frequently fail to realize, for example, that students are just as concerned about many discipline problems as they are.[8] In an extensive study of student opinions related to school discipline, DeCecco and Richards discovered that students see many behavior problems occurring because their needs and interests are ignored by teachers.[9] Students also feel that solutions to problems are imposed on them by adults rather than being negotiated. The message for DeCecco and Richards is clear — the school is not perceived to be a place where students see democracy in action.

Few people would quarrel with the fact that educators (or any occupational group, for that matter) can benefit from a greater awareness of what happens at work. In fact, much of the published educational research during the past few decades has concentrated on making teachers aware of the subtleties of classroom life. As Good, Biddle, and Brophy have observed, however, awareness alone is not enough to bring about changes in teacher behavior.[10] Teachers also need specific suggestions of ways to correct problems of which they are made aware. Awareness of problems without the tools or ideas needed to correct them actually can do more harm than good by increasing teacher frustration. The following four foci for inservice activities each involve some of these tools and ideas.

Classroom Management Skills

Classroom management refers to the provisions and procedures necessary to establish and maintain an environment in which instruction and learning can occur. Traditionally, preparing teachers in the area of classroom management has lacked precision. The past two decades, though, have witnessed increased attention to 1) locating specific teacher behaviors associated with effective management and 2) training teachers in the acquisition of these behaviors. Jacob Kounin and N. L. Gage deserve special credit for advancements in these two areas.

Kounin found that the following teacher behaviors correlated significantly with student behaviors in classrooms:

1. *Withitness and overlapping.* These dimensions deal with a teacher's communicating that she knows what is going on regarding children's behavior and with her attending to two issues simultaneously when two different issues are present.
2. *Smoothness and momentum.* These parameters measure how the teacher manages movement during recitations and at transition periods.
3. *Group alerting and accountability.* These aspects of a teacher's technique deal with the extent to which she maintains a group focus during recitations in contrast to becoming immersed in a single child.
4. *Seatwork variety and challenge.* This dimension deals with the teacher's programing learning activities with variety and intellectual challenge, especially in seat work settings [sic].[11]

In addition to the positive behaviors outlined above, Kounin isolated behaviors that teachers were advised to avoid.[12] Among these poor management practices were: 1) reprimanding the wrong child for a deviant act, 2) dealing with a less serious deviancy, while overlooking a more serious one, 3) permitting a deviancy to spread before intervening, and 4) permitting a deviancy to intensify before intervening.

Utilizing the work of Kounin and others, Gage and his colleague John Crawford designed a program to train experienced third-grade teachers to be more effective.[13] Inservice activities encompassed a series of on-site, modularized training activities led by veteran teachers. Among the 22 research-based behavioral objectives they have attempted to undertake are these five related to "behavior management and classroom discipline:"

1. Teachers should have a system of rules that allows pupils to attend to their personal and procedural needs *without* having to check with the teacher.
2. Teachers should prevent misbehaviors from continuing long

enough to increase in severity or spread to and affect other children.

3. Teachers should attempt to direct disciplinary action accurately — that is, at the child who is the primary cause of a disruption.

4. Teachers should keep "overreactions" to a minimum (even though overreactions are probably effective in stopping the misbehavior).

5. Teachers (and aides, if present) should move around the room a lot, monitor pupils' seatwork, *and* communicate to the pupils an awareness of their behavior, while also attending to their academic needs.

The two examples thus far described concentrate on general classroom management. Other efforts by behaviorists have focused on managing individual students with behavior problems. Through the systematic analysis of behavior and the application of reinforcements, teachers can be trained to eliminate inappropriate student behaviors.[14] A review of various teacher-training programs by Robert Peck and James Tucker showed that teachers could learn to utilize behavior-modification strategies successfully.[15] In a project recently undertaken by a team from the University of Louisville, for example, elementary teachers were exposed to a two-day workshop dealing with behavior-modification techniques.[16] They were taught to reward appropriate and ignore inappropriate behaviors. They also were shown how to implement time-out procedures when ignoring disruptive behavior was impractical. Over three-fifths of the children at the school where teachers had received this training were perceived to have lower levels of emotional disturbance. Children at the control school were not considered to have changed over the same period of time.

Undoubtedly, more training programs like the one described above will appear as teacher educators shift their attention from preservice to inservice education. With fewer job openings for teachers and declining enrollments, teachers are likely to be remaining in their current positions for longer periods of time. It is critical that professional development activities devoted to updating teachers' classroom management skills be created for these individuals.

Interpersonal Skills

It is not easy to separate interpersonal skills from classroom management skills. For discussion purposes, however, we shall use the former category to encompass all those behaviors related directly to the quality of communications and interactions between teachers and students. Terms like "affective education," "humanistic teaching," "sensitivity training," and "human relations" pertain to this general area.

Various studies have indicated that teachers can benefit from improvements in the way they interact with and relate to students. DeCecco and Richards, for example, contend that teachers try to control student emotions by banning their verbal expression. In so doing, they increase the likelihood of misconduct.[17] Many who observe the process of schooling have noted that teachers rarely set aside time to *listen* to students. The pressure to complete lesson plans in the allotted time apparently is too great to permit teachers to respond to student concerns as they arise. As a result, many students must keep their emotions bottled up. Ironically, teachers learn to behave in a similar fashion, though they are no more pleased at having to do so. When the situation gets intolerable enough, tempers flare and anger erupts. Lortie found that a majority of teachers are ashamed to lose their tempers with students, though they continue to do so.[18] We suspect that students are equally embarrassed when they act immaturely.

To help teachers deal with their daily problems, a group of researchers from the University of Massachusetts developed a strategy they call "social literacy training."[19] Ideally suited for ongoing inservice education, this training focuses on raising teachers' consciousness regarding the relationship between the structure of the school and their problems. Various techniques for understanding and coping with problems are generated by local social literacy groups consisting of interested teachers and trained resource people. Sometimes group members serve as peer consultants, available for classroom observation and brainstorming. Other times, they sit as a policy-advising body making recommendations to the administration. Teachers with thorny problems are referred to the group. Instead of encountering accusations and criticism, they discover an atsmophere of open inquiry and support. Two key assumptions underlying social literacy training are that 1) most people do their jobs as well as they know how and 2) spending too much time finding out who is to blame for a problem is counterproductive. The training seems to produce improved faculty relations and a more productive climate for learning.

Another inservice activity that can contribute to better teacher-student relations is the development of contingency plans. By anticipating behavior problems that might arise in class and hammering out sensible responses, teachers can avoid being caught off guard. Sometimes when teachers do not expect a particular problem to occur, they are unprepared to deal with it in a smooth, professional manner. They proceed to lose their tempers, possibly undermining their authority. Having a clear plan of action worked out in advance reduces the likelihood of class disorder. Some sample situations for which contingency plans might be useful include:

1. Student refusal in public to comply with a teacher directive.
2. Student attack on another student.
3. Student attack on teacher.
4. Appearance of an unfriendly nonstudent in class.
5. Blatant public disrespect directed at the teacher by one or several students.

Although the odds are great that these problems will not occur in a class run by a sensitive and well-organized teacher, it is always desirable to be prepared for the unexpected.

Conflict-Resolution Activities

In recent years, a shift in attitudes toward school conflicts has been detectable. Rather than attempting to suppress or prevent conflicts, educators are beginning to acknowledge the fact that conflict may be inevitable and, in certain circumstances, even desirable. How to *manage* conflicts so they do not become major disturbances is replacing conflict avoidance as a basic organizational objective.

Most teachers and administrators receive little college training relevant to conflict resolution. Hence, it will be necessary to build such training into their inservice education activities. Various conflict-resolution strategies are available for this purpose. Thomas Gordon's technique for negotiating solutions to problems between teachers and students has been discussed in a previous chapter. DeCecco and Richards recommend an approach more appropriate for conflicts of a schoolwide, as opposed to a classroom, nature. In simplest terms, their negotiation model entails three steps: 1) the statement of issues by each side made with direct, verbal expression of anger; 2) agreement by all sides on a common statement of issues — they agree to disagree; and 3) bargaining in which each side makes concessions.[20]

Academic-Intervention Skills

In contrast to the previous foci, this area does not directly entail techniques for dealing with student behavior problems. Instead, it concerns training teachers to handle course content more effectively. Many behavior problems obviously result from student frustration or anger over lack of academic success. In other instances, students grow restive because subject matter is not challenging enough.

Researchers have found, especially at the elementary school level, that some teachers are more effective in getting students to achieve than others.[21] Showing experienced teachers how they can maximize their instructional effectiveness should be a major focus of any inservice program designed to reduce behavior problems.

Arthur Whimbey, in a provocative book entitled *Intelligence Can Be Taught,* reviews a variety of programs found to have produced improvements in the academic progress of low achievers.[22] These programs demonstrated in many cases that teachers, when given the proper training and resources, could help students overcome poor preparation and low motivation levels. Whimbey's list of approaches includes teaching students how to take achievement tests, encouraging students to solve complex problems, and increasing reading comprehension. In addition, he discusses early intervention projects at the preschool level.

Gage and Crawford, in the previously cited inservice project, presented 17 objectives related to more effective academic instruction.[23] Based on analyses of the best existing research, these objectives include such items as the following:

1. Teachers should spend *at least* one-third to one-half of their time teaching larger groups of pupils (more than eight children). When they do teach smaller groups or individuals, they should take steps to make sure that the other pupils in the class have work to which they can attend.
2. Teachers should provide visual demonstrations and phonics exercises in conjunction with reading activities.

While the practice in public education has been to direct most of the funds earmarked for remedial instruction to elementary schools, school officials are advised to set aside monetary resources for secondary schools as well. It is safe to assume that junior and senior high schools will continue for many years to come to receive students lacking in the skills necessary to undertake routine coursework. These students need and deserve special programs, reading and mathematics laboratories, and teachers equipped to diagnose learning problems.

ALL-INCLUSIVE INSERVICE ACTIVITIES

> **Recommendation Number 7.4:** *Inservice for non-teaching staff members.* Nonteaching staff should receive inservice training in how to deal with student behavior problems.

The recommendations in this chapter so far have concentrated exclusively on training for classroom teachers. Nonteaching staff, ranging from administrators and secretaries to bus drivers and custodians, also need skills in how to handle student behavior problems. These individuals not only must oversee areas where misconduct can occur; they also represent people with whom many students feel comfortable. On occasion, a custodian or secretary may be able to "reach" students on whom everyone else has given up. Including these individuals in inservice activities also encourages them to feel more like an integral part of the school community, thereby increasing the likelihood that they will regard student behavior problems as *their* concern — not someone else's.

Special training for individuals who serve as disciplinarians is a particularly pressing need in many schools. Appropriate inservice

training for assistant principals, deans, special counselors, and other
school personnel who deal with student behavior problems might entail the following: interview-techniques to facilitate factfinding, as-
sessment-skills to determine whether personal counseling is required, and relevant issues concerning school law and student
rights.

Involving administrators, teachers and other school personnel in
ongoing inservice activities is critical to the success of the SMPSD.
Without provisions for continuing education, it may be difficult for
school officials to establish basic levels of understanding and competence regarding discipline. Inservice activities provide opportunities to translate recent research findings into terms that will be
meaningful in local educational contexts and to determine the bases
for cooperative action directed at the development of the school as a
rule-governed organization. In addition, well-coordinated, schoolwide inservice programs stimulate the sense of unity, common purpose and consistency so vital to any educational-improvement
effort.

Providing Professional Development Opportunities for Faculty
and Staff

Recommendations:

7.1	Annual assessment of discipline rules and procedures.
7.1.1	Assessment focuses planning of staff inservice.
7.2	Schools of education should offer relevant coursework.
7.3	Collaborative development of inservice activities.
7.4	Inservice for nonteaching staff members.

Goal Number 7: Create opportunities for faculty and staff to assess local discipline problems and acquire the skills necessary for
managing or reducing them.

Notes

1. For an example of one comprehensive inservice program, see Daniel L. Duke, "Developing a Comprehensive Inservice Program for School Improvement," *NASSP Bulletin,* 61, 408 (April 1977): 66-71.
2. Ronald L. Lien, "Professional Laboratory Programs in Russia," *The Journal of Teacher Education,* 18, 3 (Fall 1967): 319.
3. Thomas J. Coates and Carl E. Thoresen, "Teacher Anxiety: A Review with Recommendations," *Review of Educational Research,* 46, 2 (Spring 1976): 169.
4. E. K. Wickman, *Teachers and Behavior Problems* (New York: The Commonwealth Fund, 1938), p. 40.
5. Robert G. Wegmann, "Classroom Discipline: An Exercise in the Maintenance of Social Reality," *Sociology of Education,* 49, 1 (January 1976): 79.
6. Two good references for these instruments are Gary D. Borich and Susan K. Madden, *Evaluating Classroom Instruction: A Sourcebook of Instruments* (Reading, Mass.: Addison-Wesley Publishing Company, 1977) and Thomas L. Good and Jere E. Brophy, *Looking in Classrooms* (New York: Harper & Row, Publishers, 1973).
7. Daniel L. Duke, "What Can Students Tell Educators about Classroom Dynamics?" *Theory into Practice,* 16, 3 (June 1977): 262-271.
8. Daniel L. Duke, Irene A. Muzio, and Lauri Wagner, "Gathering Student Perceptions of the Classroom," *When Teachers and Researchers Cooperate,* edited by Daniel L. Duke (Stanford: Center for Educational Research at Stanford, 1977).
9. John P. DeCecco and Arlene K. Richards, *Growing Pains: Uses of School Conflict* (New York: Aberdeen Press, 1974), p. 26.
10. Thomas L. Good, Bruce J. Biddle, and Jere E. Brophy, *Teachers Make a Difference* (New York: Holt, Rinehart and Winston, 1975), p. 231.
11. Jacob S. Kounin, *Discipline and Group Management in Classrooms* (New York: Holt, Rinehart and Winston, Inc., 1970), pp. 143-144.
12. *Ibid.,* p. 82.
13. A description of the entire training program can be found in John Crawford and N. L. Gage, *"Development of a Research-Based Teacher Training Program"* (Stanford, Calif.: Stanford Center for Research and Development in Teaching, 1977).
14. For a good general reference on behavioral approaches to classroom

management, see Howard N. Sloane, *Classroom Management* (New York: John Wiley and Sons, Inc., 1976).

15. Robert F. Peck and James A. Tucker, "Research on Teacher Education," in Robert M. W. Travers (ed.), *Second Handbook of Research on Teaching* (Chicago: Rand McNally & Company, 1973), pp. 954-955.

16. Joe H. Brown, *et al.,* "The Effects of a Classroom Management Workshop on the Reduction of Children's Problematic Behaviors," *Corrective and Social Psychiatry,* 22, 2 (1976): 39-41.

17. John P. DeCecco and Arlene K. Richards, *Growing Pains: Uses of School Conflict,* (New York: Aberdeen Press, 1974), p. 189.

18. Dan C. Lortie, *Schoolteacher* (Chicago: The University of Chicago Press, 1975), p. 156.

19. Alfred Alschuler, *et al.,* Social Literacy: A Discipline Game Without Losers, *Phi Delta Kappan,* 58, 8 (April 1977): 101-109.

20. John P. DeCecco and Arlene K. Richards, *Growing Pains: Uses of School Conflict,* p. 189.

21. For an excellent general review of research on teacher effectiveness, see the previously cited book by Thomas L. Good, Bruce J. Biddle, and Jere E. Brophy, *Teachers Make a Difference.* p. 189.

22. Arthur Whimbey, *Intelligence Can Be Taught* (New York: E.P. Dutton & Co., Inc., 1975).

23. John Crawford and N. L. Gage, "Development of a Research-Based Teacher Training Program" (Stanford: Center for Research and Development in Teaching, 1977).

PART **III**

An Action Agenda

11

Implementing the SMPSD

THE IDEAS PRESENTED IN this book constitute an approach to the management of student behavior problems on a school-wide rather than classroom-by-classroom basis. As a result, the task of implementing the SMPSD is much more ambitious than the process of getting one teacher to alter his or her style of classroom management. In many cases, implementation will require basic changes in school organization — in who makes decisions and how they are made, rules and sanctions, and grievance procedures. Changes of this magnitude require careful thought and planning. The sorry history of many previous efforts to improve schooling attests to the difficulty of the undertaking.

One way that organizational development specialists attempt to reduce the likelihood of failure is to encourage innovators to think of organizational change as a series of steps, each of which requires careful deliberation. An additional characteristic of a systematic approach is that it should provide for cyclical review and revision so that the new system can continue to respond to changing organizational realities. Implementing the SMPSD may be viewed as a three-part process, beginning with a preliminary assessment of school needs and resources, moving on to planning and enactment of the plan, and continuing with review and revision (see Figure 2). Although we shall discuss separately each phase of this process, in reality the phases may overlap. Systematic change is a continuous process of creation, selection and adaptation to meet the needs of those affected by the change.

PHASE I: PRELIMINARY ASSESSMENT

No effort to undertake organizational change should begin without some attempt to gather information on perceived needs and the organizational climate for change. Do members of the school community agree that change is necessary? What resources are they willing to commit to the effort? How have previous change efforts fared? What can be learned from these experiences?

Questions such as these imply that no innovation ever begins at point zero. Those who will be expected to undertake the change-effort have beliefs and attitudes that will guide their behavior during implementation. Their beliefs and attitudes have been influenced, to some extent, by their experiences with previous innovations. As the saying goes, to ignore the past is to be condemned to repeat it.

A useful tool for guiding the preliminary assessment of perceived needs and school climate is the Duke Assessment of School Discipline (DASD. See Addenda). The DASD is designed to highlight needs in areas that correspond to components of the SMPSD. Discussion of the findings of the DASD is apt to reveal that many people have different perceptions of the need for change. Everyone may not feel the same urgency about change, but there should be some agreement concerning what needs changing.

Surveys are only one possible source of assessment data. Interviews with representative teachers, students, staff members, and parents can be another valuable source of information. Careful observation of campus activities, student-student/student-teacher interactions, and the appearance of the campus (i.e., amount of trash in hallways, graffiti on the walls, damaged student lockers) can also provide valuable clues to the nature of the existing environment, the need for change, and the potential for improvement.

Schools where the level of serious student behavior problems is high often show considerable consensus on the need for change. Those who recognize the need, however, may disagree radically as to what to change and whether or not a particular change will bring improvement. The importance of organization members' attitudes toward change has begun to be recognized and studied by researchers.[1] Zaltman and Duncan have identified five key factors in assessing the climate for change: perceived need for change, openness to change, potential for change, perceived control over the change process, and commitment to change.[2]

Each factor can affect the organization's ability to engage in successful change-efforts, but the critical elements are the relationships between factors when the need for change is high. Zaltman and Duncan contend that the greater the perceived need for change, the less likely people are to perceive a potential for change, feel an openness to change, or feel that they can participate in change decision-making.[3]

A school besieged with student behavior problems may be in great need of change; but if staff and parents do not believe that real change is possible, the effort may be doomed to failure before it begins. The first task in such a case would be to change negative attitudes. Only after accomplishing this task should efforts be directed to systematic planning.

Although we cannot specify the "necessary" preconditions for successful implementation of the SMPSD at every school, we offer the following questions as possibilities for Phase I assessment:

Need for change:

Do most of the members of the school community (teachers, staff, parents and students) recognize that student behavior is a problem at our school?

Yes   No

Are these same people ready to consider changes in school organization?

Yes   No

Change in the past:

Have many members of the current staff participated in past efforts directed at changing student behavior?

Yes   No

Were past efforts successful?

Yes   No

Do those who participated in past change-efforts believe that their time and effort were well-spent?

Yes   No

Commitment to change:

Are most of the members of the school community willing to commit time and energy to implementing a comprehensive program?

           Yes   No

Are individuals willing to change some of their own procedures and behaviors in order to accommodate the needs of a school-wide program?

           Yes   No

We advise that these or related questions be explored initially in small groups where individuals can feel comfortable expressing concerns. If responses to these basic questions are positive, work can begin on Phase II of implementation. Negative replies do not necessarily mean that change is impossible. They may suggest, however, that the timing is inappropriate for implementation and that preliminary work on developing positive attitudes is required.

PHASE II: PLANNING AND ENACTMENT OF THE PLAN

Once Phase I assessment has determined need for change and a relatively favorable climate for it, actual planning can begin. One of the first tasks for planners is to study the goals of the SMPSD and determine which match school needs. Realistic goal setting and careful sequencing of target goals are very important.

Certain goals of the SMPSD may initially be unrealistic for some schools. The most pressing problem is not necessarily the one to address first. Typically the most pressing problem also is the one requiring the greatest investment of time, energy, imagination, and resources. To commence with an attack on such a problem may ensure that school personnel have an opportunity to fail before succeeding. A wiser course of action may be to start with a goal that can be easily achieved, saving the tougher goals until a few successes have been recorded.

Among the SMPSD goals that may be most easily achieved are the development of a uniform set of school rules, the establishment

Figure 2

**Three Phases of Implementation for the
Systematic Management Plan
for School Discipline**

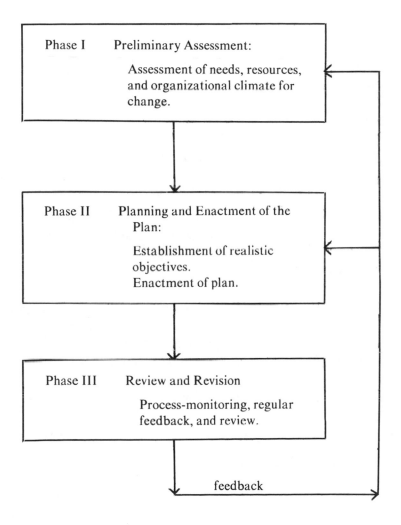

of a system for the ongoing collection of data on student behavior problems, and the planning of staff-development activities. Goals that may be more dependent on the time-consuming process of trustbuilding include involving parents in school discipline and developing team troubleshooting capabilities.

The process of matching school needs with SMPSD goals undoubtedly will encounter some resistance. To assist implementers, we have anticipated some typical concerns likely to be voiced by teachers, staff, students, and parents. The concerns are related to one component of the SMPSD — the development of the school as a rule-governed organization. Suggested responses to these concerns follow each example.

Teacher Concern: Working with students on school rules takes time away from learning the basic skills.

Suggested Reply: Learning to live in the rule-governed society of which we are a part certainly is *basic* to human existence.

Teacher Concern: I don't have time to prepare extra units on school rules or test students on their knowledge of them.

Suggested Reply: You shouldn't perceive this to be another "add-on." Making students aware of school rules ultimately should save much of the time you ordinarily spend on disruptive, recalcitrant students who feign ignorance of the rules.

Teacher Concern: Collaborative development of rules and student participation in decision-making means that teacher authority will be further eroded. We will have to give up some of our power to the students, and we have little enough already.

Suggested Reply: Implementing a comprehensive plan such as the SMPSD does not mean playing a zero-sum game. No one has to "lose" so that others can gain greater participation.

Administrative   We need more rules, not less. The kids aren't
Concern: following the rules we have already.

Suggested Reply: Exactly the reason that "less is more" in this case. We need to concentrate on the rules we can enforce and on the ones really important to all of us within the school community.

Parent Concern: I want my children to be treated fairly and consistently. My children shouldn't be punished for an offense unless others are.

Suggested Reply: You have identified one of the reasons that we are attempting to develop a schoolwide policy regarding student behavior. In this way, we can encourage consistent and fair rule-enforcement for each student.

Student Concern: Rules are just made for the benefit of adults. You know they aren't really going to let kids have any say on important rules, the ones that are different for kids and teachers. Nobody ever worries about kids getting their stuff ripped off or being hassled by older kids.

Suggested Reply: We are trying to eliminate the double standards you're complaining about by working together to develop rules, sanctions, and rewards. If we work together to develop a list of school rules and everyone knows them, we can devote time and attention to problems that most concern students as well as those that bother adults.

Understanding and dealing with the concerns of school community members is essential to the implementation of the SMPSD, because to do so requires a great deal of collaborative work and shared decision-making. Implementers must possess some skill in interpersonal communication and be sensitive to the feelings of all participants. School officials should be committed to sharing some authority over decision-making with teachers, staff, and students. Otherwise, the likelihood is minimal of getting the quality of participation needed from these individuals in order for the plan to succeed.

From the delineation of guidelines for classroom behavior to the determination of rewards for positive behavior, the collaboration processes called for in the SMPSD require skill, patience, and careful orchestration. Inservice training in decision making may be necessary. Among the potential pitfalls of shared decision-making that must be dealt with are the following:

1. The process takes time, and one person's uncooperativeness or lack of knowledge can prolong the decision.
2. Group work requires a high degree of skill on the part of the facilitator(s).
3. The decision can be reduced to the least objectionable alternative.
4. The process may lead to "block voting" whereby group members are divided into separate camps.[4]

An honest commitment to developing competent decision-makers at every level of the school organization will do much to encourage involvement in the process of organizational change. Students and staff alike can gain a much needed sense of "ownership" in and responsibility for their school. Once the groundwork has been laid for collaborative work, planning meetings will run more smoothly and tend to be more productive.

DEVELOPING THE LOCAL SMPSD PLAN

We have described a series of recommendations and best existing-practices that indicate how the intent of the SMPSD recommendations might be actualized. At best, however, these are guidelines, which must be modified for each school site. For example, placing a counselor in a school exercise-room may be an excellent way to reach students *if* the school has such a facility, but is obviously impossible otherwise. Teaming truant students with peers who attend school regularly may be a problem because of bussing patterns in a given school district. Some schools might not be able to afford the cost of hiring community resource persons. Each of the SMPSD recommendations must be adjusted to the available resources and idiosyncratic features of individual schools.

1. Issue or topic under consideration in this meeting
2. The central points made in discussion
3. Specific decisions made in the meeting
4. Assignment of responsibility for carrying out specific decisions (and reporting back to the group).

Collaborative decision-making is an essential characteristic of the SMPSD. Sharing authority in decision-making does not mean, however, that strong leadership is not required. Effective leadership, in fact, is necessary to maintain focus on the critical issues (easily lost in the detail of the project-planning) and to guide the efforts of the many constituent groups involved in the process. One of the major findings of the National Institute of Education's Safe School Study was that the quality of school leadership was directly related to the level of school violence and vandalism.[5]

PHASE III: REVIEW AND REVISION

Once efforts to implement the SMPSD have begun, it is time to consider the third phase of the process. This step, often abandoned when time is short, calls for cyclical review and revision of the implementation process. Even the best plans may need modification in the ever-changing "real" world. Providing objective feedback on performance to individuals involved in implementation can be a vital component of quality control efforts.

The process of program review may address questions such as the following: How do we know that our objectives are being achieved? Have the criteria by which we determine program-success changed? How are the individuals responsible for implementing the plan coping with their new demands? Are the resources originally available for implementation still available? Can new resources be obtained?

These and other review-questions can be tackled in a variety of ways. Short, early-morning or after-school meetings may prove adequate for information sharing. The survey instruments and interviews utilized in Phase I may be readministered in order for individuals to see whether their perceptions have changed.

Time must be set aside to analyze feedback and revise the original plans. School personnel should be warned early in the implementation process that periodically time will be needed for review and revision. Otherwise, they may resent the new time-imposition and begin to question the value of the original planning sessions. School personnel are no different from anyone else to the extent that they prefer to know what to expect when they embark on a new course — even if the expectation concerns additional effort and time.

A theme throughout the discussion of the three stages of implementation has been the importance of allocating sufficient time for careful thought and planning. So vital is this factor that the next section is devoted exclusively to a discussion of time.

No Substitute for Time

Individuals responsible for dealing with student behavior problems often complain that they are too busy coping with daily emergencies to engage in systematic planning, decision-making, or review. These persons are indisputably busy, but their contention may nonetheless be shortsighted. Charles Hummel observes that

The important task rarely must be done today, or even this week. The urgent task calls for instant action. The momentary appeal of these tasks seems irresistible and they devour our energy. But in the light of time's perspective their deceptive prominence fades. With a sense of loss we recall the important tasks pushed aside. We realize we've become slaves to the tyranny of the urgent.[6]

The first line of defense against the "tyranny of the urgent" is awareness. If school personnel are made aware that several years may be required to fully implement the SMPSD, they are less likely to be disappointed when long-standing problems do not evaporate overnight. Second in importance is motivation. It is unrealistic to expect most teachers to volunteer large portions of their free time for committee work without some incentives. If student behavior problems are serious enough, perhaps the possibility of reducing them will be sufficiently motivating to spur faculty involvement. In many instances, though, teachers may need the inducement of released time, lighter teaching-loads, or monetary remuneration.

Schools are made up of various role groups, each of which may possess a different notion of the amount of time required to complete a given set of tasks. Sarason has observed that it is necessary to compare

the time perspective of the agents of change with that of those who are the targets, and that of those who will, in one way or another, participate in the (change) process. This comparison is crucial because if, as is usually the case, the differences in time perspective are great, the seeds of conflict and disillusionment are already in the soil.[7]

Time-needs of parents, students, and staff vary, even as does their understanding of student behavior problems. Realistic time-lines are essential and modifications must be communicated to participants regularly. In planning to implement the SMPSD, consideration should be given to how much time can be made available for each of the following activities:

1. Collection of data on student behavior
2. Analysis of data on student behavior
3. Reporting of data on student behavior to school personnel
4. Publicizing of data analyses
5. Daily administrative briefings and debriefings
6. Developing and utilizing conflict-resolution procedures
7. Faculty troubleshooting meetings and case conferences
8. Guidance department office hours after school and during evenings
9. Daily phone contacts with parents, when needed
10. Daily monitoring of absent students
11. Orientation of new teachers and students to school rules
12. Rule-setting meetings
13. Parent-education programs
14. Faculty-staff inservice programs
15. Curriculum development
16. Testing students on school rules

Some of the time required for these activities can be obtained through more efficient use of personnel and the elimination of "make-work" assignments. For example, unenforceable or outdated rules can be abolished. Beyond a certain point, though, new ideas must be considered. Moving to block scheduling or encouraging team teaching can provide teachers with the flexibility necessary to deal with student concerns as they arise. Hiring a secretary to be responsible for collecting and processing disciplinary data can free administrators to spend more time listening to complaints and mediating conflict-resolution procedures. Convincing teachers that school rules and student conduct are subjects worthy of consideration within the regular academic curriculum may reduce the amount of time spent on special assemblies, hearings, and general rule enforcement.

Ultimately, of course, the SMPSD is designed to save time. If we can assume that teachers and administrators spend too much of their time (not to mention energy) reacting to or suffering from behavior problems, then the possibility of decreasing this time more than justifies the initial work required to implement the SMPSD. The *complete* elimination of student behavior problems is unlikely, of course, no matter what plan is implemented. Confronting student problems and maintaining the school's credibility as a rule-governed organization must be regarded as ongoing activities, deserving some continuing output of time and effort. New teachers should be counseled to anticipate spending a portion of their instructional time listening to student concerns, negotiating solutions to differences of opinion, and teaching students about rules. In short, the probability of successful implementation of the SMPSD is directly proportional to the quality, if not the amount, of time committed to that purpose.

CONCLUSION

The preceding pages contain a variety of recommendations, perhaps more than can be easily absorbed in one reading. The number and scope of the recommendations may seem overwhelming. Those who have illusions, however, that improving the school's ability to deal effectively and humanely with student behavior problems is an effortless undertaking will quickly find themselves "dis-illusioned."

What we have proposed in this book is nothing less than a restructuring of school organization to permit educators and students to interact more productively and enjoyably. A major belief that underlies our recommendations is that schools exist to serve students, not vice versa. If some students are not behaving appropriately, they may be communicating the fact that the school is no longer perceived to be serving their needs. Since it is unrealistic to expect any school always to respond equally well to the needs of every student, educators must antitipate a certain number of behavior problems, no matter how hard they labor. By developing mechanisms for monitoring and resolving these problems on a collaborative basis, the SMPSD tries to prevent teacher frustration without sacrificing basic student rights.

One recommendation must supercede all of the previous ones. In fact, most of the SMPSD would be unnecessary if members of the school community could adhere to this principle consistently. It is embodied in the Golden Rule: "Do unto others as you would have them do unto you." The exigencies of daily life in schools and the ways they are organized sometimes prevent members of the school community from acting on the principle. More than anything else, we intend the SMPSD as a way to modify school organization in order to encourage people to consider others.

Notes

1. Seymour Sarason, *The Culture of the School and the Problem of Change,* (Boston: Allyn and Bacon, Inc., 1971), pp. 20-24.
2. Gerald Zaltman and Robert Duncan, *Strategies for Planned Change* (New York: John Wiley & Sons, 1977), p. 243.
3. *Ibid.,* p. 79.
4. Adapted from Jean Rosaler, *How to Make the Best School Site Council in the World,* (Sacramento: California State Department of Education, 1979), p. 64.

5. National Institute of Education, *Violent Schools-Safe Schools* (Washington, D.C.: U.S. Government Printing Office, 1978), p. 169.

6. Charles Hummel's remark is quoted in R. Alec Mackenzie, *The Time Trap* (New York: McGraw-Hill Book Company, 1972), p. 43.

7. Sarason, p. 219.

Appendices
References
Index

Comprehensive List of SMPSD Goals and Recommendations

Goal Number 1: Create an awareness on the part of all who work and study in the school that it is an organization governed by rules.

> **Recommendation Number 1.1:** *Collaborative development of school rules.* School and classroom rules as well as the consequences for disobeying them should be decided collaboratively among teachers, students, administrators, and parents.
> **Recommendation Number 1.2:** *Rules-related content incorporated in academic curriculum.* Skills, attitudes, and content related to school rules, rule-making, and the nature of rule-governed organizations should be incorporated into the regular academic curriculum of the school.
> **Recommendation Number 1.3:** *Student instruction on school rules.* Students should be taught about school rules and the consequences for disobeying them.
> **Recommendation Number 1.3.1:** *Regular testing of knowledge of school rules.* Students should be tested on school rules and the consequences for disobeying them.
> **Recommendation Number 1.4:** *Student participation in rule-making regarding adult behavior.* Students should have opportunities to deliberate rules governing teacher behavior.
> **Recommendation Number 1.5:** *Frequent publicizing of school rules.* School rules and the consequences for disobeying them should be publicized widely and updated regularly.
> **Recommendation Number 1.6:** *Orientation of transfer students.* Special arrangements should be made to orient all transfer students to school rules.
> **Recommendation Number 1.7:** *Enforcement facilitated by minimum number of rules.* The number of school rules should be kept to a minimum to facilitate consistent enforcement and student retention.
> **Recommendation Number 1.8:** *Procedures for consistent rule application and enforcement.* Provisions should be made for the encouragement of consistent and fair rule enforcement

and the resolution of routine problems involving inconsistencies and unfair treatment.

Goal Number 2: Collect, maintain, and utilize data on student behavior to improve school discipline.

> **Recommendation Number 2.1:** *Development of standard reporting procedures.* Standard procedures for reporting behavior problems should be developed.
>
> **Recommendation Number 2.2:** *Allocation of responsibility for data control.* One or two school employees should be given responsibility for receiving, storing, and periodically disseminating disciplinary data.
>
> **Recommendation Number 2.3:** *Regular review of collected data.* Data on student behavior should be shared with teachers and others in the school on a regular basis. Time should be allocated so that data can be reviewed and suggestions can be made about how to improve school discipline.
>
> **Recommendation Number 2.4:** *Functional use of data in policymaking.* Data on student behavior should be used in the formulation of schoolwide objectives related to improvements in discipline.
>
> **Recommendation Number 2.5:** *Public reporting of discipline data.* Data on school discipline should be reported regularly to the Board of Education and the general public.

Goal Number 3: Provide opportunities for those who work and study in school to express their concerns and problems in a supportive atmosphere.

> **Recommendation Number 3.1:** *Situation specificity.* In any process of conflict resolution in school, educators should attempt to deal only with the specific situation at hand.
>
> **Recommendation Number 3.2:** *Speedy action necessary.* Conflicts that arise in the classroom should be handled between the teacher and the student(s) involved as soon after they occur as possible.

Recommendation Number 3.2.1: *Private conferences.* Conflict resolution procedures should take place on an individual basis and in private.

Recommendation Number 3.2.2: *Informational hearings.* Students accused of misconduct should have an opportunity (hearing) to explain how they perceive what occurred and why.

Recommendation Number 3.2.3: *Negotiated problem-solving.* Solutions to conflicts should be negotiated between teacher and student(s).

Recommendation Number 3.3: *Trained resource persons.* When conflicts cannot be resolved at the classroom level between teacher and student, resource people should be available to hear both sides of the issue and assist in negotiating a settlement.

Recommendation Number 3.3.1: *Collaborative selection of resource persons.* In order for the resource persons to enjoy maximum credibility, students and teachers should be involved in their selection.

Recommendation Number 3.3.2: *Impartial functioning of resource persons.* A resource person should regard his or her primary functions as 1) providing a hearing for the conflicting parties and 2) negotiating a solution to the conflict that is acceptable to them. Under no circumstances should he or she serve as an agent of the administration concerned with enforcing school rules or meting out punishment.

Recommendation Number 3.4: *Student participation in problem-solving.* Opportunities should be provided for students to participate in the conflict-resolution process.

Goal Number 4: In as many cases as possible, shift responsibility for diagnosing and managing serious behavior problems from individuals to teams.

Recommendation Number 4.1: *Anticipation of problems by troubleshooting teams.* Teachers working with the same students should form grade-level teams. These teams should convene periodically for troubleshooting — anticipating problems before they become major upsets.

Recommendation Number 4.1.1: *Specificity of discussion.* Discussions must involve references to specific students rather than broad statements, vague feelings, or anecdotes.

Recommendation Number 4.1.2: *Need for confidentiality.* All discussions must be kept in strictest confidence.

Recommendation Number 4.1.3: *Planning of specific actions.* For each student discussed during a troubleshooting session, a specific plan of action must be adopted before the session ends.

Recommendation Number 4.1.4: *Delegation of responsibility.* One person must assume responsibility for seeing that the plan of action is implemented. Responsibilities should be distributed equitably (i.e., counselors should not always be selected).

Recommendation Number 4.1.5: *Regular feed-back on cases.* The individual responsible for seeing that the plan of action is implemented must report back to the group at the next session about its success.

Recommendation Number 4.1.6: *Documentation of proceedings.* Minutes should be taken of all troubleshooting session proceedings.

Recommendation Number 4.2: *Follow up case conferences.* Case conferences should be scheduled for any student who continues to experience problems after a plan of action has been developed at a troubleshooting session.

Recommendation Number 4.3: *Inventory of potential resources.* An inventory should be made of potential resource persons who would be willing to assist in case conferences.

Recommendation Number 4.3.1: *Informal resource persons' meetings.* An effort should be made to have the resource persons meet together periodically on an informal basis to discuss general concerns and school discipline policies.

Recommendation Number 4.4: *Employment of additional resource personnel.* When possible, school officials should locate funds to hire special resource people to participate on a regular basis in case conferences and other team activities.

Recommendation Number 4.5: *Utilization of existing staff in new roles.* New ways of utilizing existing staff more effectively in collaborative efforts to reduce behavior problems should be considered.

Recommendation Number 4.6: *Student membership on problem-solving teams.* Students should be regarded as essential members of any team designed to work on improving school discipline.

Recommendation 4.7: *Initiation of special task forces for acute problems.* Special task forces should be used to attack acute or special problems requiring intensive, short-term collaboration, definite decisions, and a relatively high degree of local publicity.

Goal Number 5: Involve parents in the diagnosis and resolution of student behavior problems as well as in prevention programs.

Recommendation Number 5.1: *Parent involvement in school rule revision.* Periodically parents should be involved in reviewing and revising school rules.

Recommendation Number 5.2: *Annual report to parents on discipline policies.* Parents should be notified annually of all school rules and disciplinary policies.

Recommendation Number 5.3: *Provision for parent education.* The school should provide opportunities for parents to gain new skills and knowledge related to child-rearing and behavior problems.

Recommendation Number 5.4: *Immediate parent notification of problems.* Parents should be informed of problems involving their children as soon as possible. Direct contact or contact over the phone always is preferable to written notification. When the latter course of action must be followed, letters should be mailed special delivery (return receipt requested) or entrusted to a courier.

Recommendation Number 5.4.1: *Verification of student absences.*

Parents should be contacted on a routine basis to verify absences.

Recommendation Number 5.4.2: *Daily telephoning hour.* An hour each day should be set aside for telephone calls to parents whose children are beginning to experience problems in school. Responsibility for home phoning can be shared among administrators, counselors, and perhaps a trusted executive secretary.

Recommendation Number 5.5: *Parent involvement in problem resolution.* Parents should be involved in resolving major discipline problems involving their children.

Goal Number 6: Rather than trying to curtail behavior problems simply by increasing punishments, reinforce regularly those student behaviors that contribute to a healthy school environment.

Recommendation Number 6.1: *Privileges for positive behavior.* Students who regularly obey school rules should receive certain privileges not accorded students who do not obey rules.

Recommendation Number 6.2: *Student participation in the determination of rewards and sanctions.* Students should be involved in determining the privileges for good behavior as well as the consequences for disobeying rules.

Recommendation Number 6.3: *Provision for alternative learning environments.* Schools should provide optional learning environments for students needing more personalized attention and less rigid behavior expectations.

Recommendation Number 6.4: *Provision for short-term behavior improvement programs.* Schools should provide short-term programs focusing on behavior improvement for students temporarily unable or unwilling to conform to school rules.

Recommendation Number 6.5: *Development of positive peer group influence.* School officials should work with students, particularly student leaders, to develop the peer group as a force acting to reinforce positive behavior.

Recommendation Number 6.6: *Avoidance of corporal punish-*

ment. Teachers and administrators should avoid the use of physical punishment to correct student behavior.

Goal Number 7: Create opportunities for faculty and staff to assess local discipline problems and acquire the skills necessary for managing or reducing them.

> **Recommendation Number 7.1:** *Annual assessment of discipline rules and procedures.* Part of spring wrap-up acitvities should involve assessing the effectiveness of school rules and disciplinary procedures during the year just completed and agreeing on guidelines for the coming year.
>
> **Recommendation Number 7.1.1:** *Assessment focuses planning of staff inservice.* For areas where problems are found to exist, plans should be made for appropriate inservice activities during the coming school year.
>
> **Recommendation Number 7.2:** *Schools of education should offer relevant coursework.* Pressure should be exerted on schools of education to offer more courses devoted to student behavior problems and school discipline.
>
> **Recommendation Number 7.3:** *Collaborative development of inservice activities.* Inservice activities concerning how to deal effectively with student behavior problems should be undertaken collaboratively by school administrators and teachers.
>
> **Recommendation Number 7.4:** *Inservice for non-teaching staff members.* Non-teaching staff should receive inservice training in how to deal with student behavior problems.
>
> **Recommendation Number 8:** Do unto others as you would have them do unto you.

Duke Assessment of School Discipline*

This assessment form is designed to facilitate the process of planning the implementation of the Systematic Management Plan for School Discipline. The statements that follow each have a five-point rating scale beneath them. *Please circle the number you feel best describes the situation at your school.* Thank you for your cooperation.

Do Not Write Below This Line. Go To The Next Page.

Subtotals: 1. Rule-Governed Organization   _____

2. Data Collection   _____

3. Conflict Resolution   _____

4. Team Approach   _____

5. Parental Involvement   _____

6. Rewards   _____

7. Professional Development   _____

TOTAL   _____

*A Note on the Use of the DASD
The Duke Assessment of School Discipline was developed as a guide for those who wish to conduct a status check of school discipline. It is not "standardized" nor are the weights assigned to particular items necessarily equivalent. Mean scores of three or lower on particular items, however, do suggest areas in need of attention.

1. The School As a Rule-Governed Organization

1.1 School and classroom rules are decided collaboratively among students, teachers, and administrators.

5	4	3	2	1

All of the time	Some of the time	Little or none of the time

1.1.1 Parents participate in making school and classroom rules.

5	4	3	2	1

All of the time	Some of the time	Little or none of the time

1.2 Skills, attitudes, and content related to school rules and student behavior are incorporated into the regular academic curriculum.

5	4	3	2	1

In most courses	In some courses	In few or no courses

1.3 Students are tested on school rules and the consequences for disobeying them.

5	4	3	2	1

All students are tested annually	Some students are tested	Students are not tested as a rule

1.4 Students participate in developing rules governing teacher behavior.

5	4	3	2	1

Often	Some of the time	Never

1.5 School rules and the consequences for disobeying them are publicized widely.

	5	4	3	2	1

Posted in halls, class-rooms, etc.	Printed in hand-books	Not avail-able

1.6 School rules are re-assessed.

	5	4	3	2	1

Annually	Occasion-ally	Rarely

1.7 Special arrangements are made to orient transfer students to school rules.

	5	4	3	2	1

In all cases	Sometimes	Rarely

1.8 Provisions exist to encourage consistent enforcement of school rules and the fair application of justice.

	5	4	3	2	1

Formal pro-visions exist	Informal processes exist	No pro-visions exist

Additional Questions

A. Does a list of school rules exist?
   YES   NO   UNSURE

B. If a list of school rules exists, how many rules are contained in the list?   _____

2. Adequate Data Collection

2.1 Routine procedures for reporting behavior problems exist.

5	4	3	2	1

Procedures exist and are used all of the time	Procedures exist and are used sometimes	Routine procedures do not exist

2.2. School personnel are responsible for receiving, storing, and disseminating data on student behavior.

5	4	3	2	1

Data is regularly processed	Data is processed on occasion	Data is not processed at all

2.3. Data on student behavior is shared with school personnel.

5	4	3	2	1

Regularly	Occasion- ally	Rarely

2.4 Schoolwide objectives related to student behavior exist.

5	4	3	2	1

Objectives exist and are pursued	Objectives exist on paper	No formal objectives exist

2.5 Data on school discipline is reported to the public.

5	4	3	2	1

Regularly	Occasion- ally	Rarely

3. Conflict-Resolution Provisions

3.1 Classroom conflicts are handled between the teacher and the student(s) involved.

5	4	3	2	1
Regularly		Occasion- ally		Rarely

3.2 Teachers negotiate solutions to classroom conflicts with the student(s) involved.

5	4	3	2	1
Regularly		Occasion- ally		Rarely

3.3 When conflicts cannot be resolved at the classroom level, resource people are available to listen to both sides.

5	4	3	2	1
Regularly		Occasion- ally		Rarely

3.4 Students are involved as mediators/arbitrators in the conflict resolution process.

5	4	3	2	1
Regularly		Occasion- ally		Rarely

4. Team Approach to Improved Student Behavior

4.1 Teachers meet in troubleshooting sessions to identify students who are beginning to experience behavior problems. The teachers develop corrective strategies.

5	4	3	2	1
Regularly		Occasion- ally		Rarely

4.2 Case conferences are scheduled for any students experiencing chronic behavior problems.

5	4	3	2	1
Regularly		Occasion-ally		Rarely

4.3 Efforts are made to involve community resource people (pediatricians, ministers, probation officials, social workers, etc.) in dealing with students experiencing chronic behavior problems.

5	4	3	· 2	1
Regularly		Occasion-ally		Rarely

5. Parental Involvement

5.1 Parents are notified of school rules.

5	4	3	2	1
All parents notified annually		Parents notified irregularly		Parents are not notified

5.2 The school provides opportunities for parents to gain new skills in dealing with their children.

5	4	3	2	1
Numerous opportunities are available		A few parent programs		No parent education program

5.3 Parents are notified when their children encounter discipline problems at school.

5	4	3	2	1
Parents are always notified immediately		Parents are sometimes notified		Parents are rarely notified

5.4 Parents are contacted to verify student absences.

5	4	3	2	1
In all cases		Occasionally		Rarely

5.5 Parents are involved in resolving discipline problems involving their children.

5	4	3	2	1
In all cases		Occasionally		Rarely

6. Rewards and Punishments

6.1 Students who regularly obey school rules receive special privileges.

5	4	3	2	1
In all cases		Occasionally		Rarely

6.2 Students are involved in determining the privileges for those who regularly obey school rules.

5	4	3	2	1
Students are regularly involved		Students are sometimes involved		Students are never involved

6.3 Optional or alternative learning environments are available for students with special interests or learning needs.

5	4	3	2	1
Many options are available		A few options are available		No options are available

6.4 Short-term programs focusing on behavior improvement are available for students with discipline problems (i.e., in-school suspension, after-school class on behavior improvement, Saturday school, etc.).

5	4	3	2	1
A variety of programs		One or two programs		No programs

6.5 School officials work with student leaders to encourage good behavior among all students.

5	4	3	2	1
Regularly		Occasion-ally		Rarely

6.6 Corporal punishment is employed.

5	4	3	2	1
Rarely or never		Occasion-ally		Regularly

7. Professional Development Related to Discipline

7.1 Efforts are made prior to the summer recess to assess school discipline during the year.

5	4	3	2	1
Annually		Every few years		Rarely, if ever

7.2 Inservice programs dealing with topics related to student behavior problems are available.

5	4	3	2	1

Regularly   Occasion-   Rarely,
                        ally   if ever

7.3 Nonteaching (non-professional) staff members participate in
inservice activities concerning student behavior
problems.

5	4	3	2	1

Whenever   On some   Never
programs   occasions
are avail-
able

References

Alschuler, Alfred, *et al.* "Social Literacy: A Discipline Game Without Losers," *Phi Delta Kappan,* 58, 8 (April 1977): 606-609.

W. C. Becker, *et al.* "The Contingent Use of Teacher Attention and Praise in Reducing Classroom Behavior Problems," *The Journal of Special Education,* 1, 3 (Spring 1967): 287-307.

Borich, Gary D., and Madden, Susan K. *Evaluating Classroom Instruction: A Sourcebook of Instruments* (Reading, Mass.: Addison-Wesley Publishing Company, 1977).

Bridge, R. Gary. "Parent Participation in School Innovations," *Teachers College Record,* 77, 3 (February 1976): 366-384.

Bronfenbrenner, Urie. *Two Worlds of Childhood: U.S. and U.S.S.R.* (New York: Pocket Books, 1973).

Brookover, W. B. "Self-Concept of Ability and School Achievement" in H. L. Miller (ed.), *Education for the Disadvantaged* (New York: The Free Press, 1967).

Brown, Catherine Caldwell. "It Changed My Life," *Psychology Today,* 10, 6 (November 1976): 47-57.

Brown, Joe H., *et al.* "The Effects of a Classroom Management Workshop on the Reduction of Children's Problematic Behaviors," *Corrective and Social Psychiatry,* 22, 2 (1976): 39-41.

Buxton, Thomas H. and Prichard, Keith W. "Student Perceptions of Teacher Violations of Human Rights," *Phi Delta Kappan,* 55, 1 (September 1973): 66-69.

Byerly, Carl L. "A School Curriculum for Prevention and Remediation of Deviancy" in William W. Wattenberg (ed.), *Social Deviancy among Youth,* The Sixty-fifth Yearbook of the National Society for the Study of Education, Part 1 (Chicago: The University of Chicago Press, 1966), pp. 221-257.

Clarizio, Harvey F., and McCoy, George F. *Behavior Disorders in Children,* Second Edition (New York: Thomas Y. Crowell Company, 1976).

Coates, Thomas J., and Thoresen, Carl E. "Teacher Anxiety: A Review with Recommendations," *Review of Educational Research,* 46, 3 (Spring 1976): 159-184.

Cohen, Elizabeth G., Intili, Jo-Ann K., and Robbins, Susan H. "Task and Authority: A Sociological View of Classroom Management" in Daniel L. Duke (ed.), *Classroom Management,* The Seventy-Eighth Yearbook of the National Society for the Study of Education, Part II (Chicago: The University of Chicago Press, 1979).

Corwin, Ronald G. *Militant Professionalism* (New York: Appleton-Century Crofts, 1970), p. 355.

Crawford, John, and Gage, N. L. *Development of a Research-Based Teacher Training Program* (Stanford: Stanford Center for Research and Development in Teaching, 1977).

Davies, Don, ed. *Schools Where Parents Make a Difference* (Boston: The Institute for Responsive Education, 1976).

Dececco, John P., and Richards, Arlene K. *Growing Pains: Uses of School Conflict* (New York: Aberdeen Press, 1974).

Dinkmeyer, Don C. "The Parent 'C' Group," *Personnel and Guidance Journal,* 51, 4 (December 1973): 252-256.

Dreikurs, Rudolf, and Grey, Loren. *A New Approach to Discipline: Logical Consequences* (New York: Hawthorn Books, Inc., 1968).

Duff, Charles F., *et al.* "Acceptance and Rejection of Rules Governing Student Conduct," *Phi Delta Kappan,* 58, 6 (February 1977): 502.

Duke, Daniel L., and Meckel, Adrienne M. "Disciplinary Rules in American Schools" (Submitted for publication).

Duke, Daniel L. "Adults Can Be Discipline Problems Too!" *Psychology in the Schools,* 15, 4 (October 1978): 522-528.

———. "Can the Curriculum Contribute to Resolving the Educator's Discipline Dilemma?" *Action in Teacher Education,* 1, 2 (Fall-Winter, 1978): 17-36.

———, (ed.). *Classroom Management.* The Seventy-Eighth Yearbook of the National Society for the Study of Education, Part II (Chicago: University of Chicago Press, 1979).

———. "Developing a Comprehensive Inservice Program for School Improvement," *NASSP Bulletin,* 61, 408 (April 1977): 66-71.

———. "How Administrators View the Crisis in School Discipline," *Phi Delta Kappan,* 59, 5 (January 1978): 325-330.

———. "Looking at the School as a Rule-Governed Organization," *The Journal of Research and Development in Education,* 11, 4 (Summer 1978): 116-126.

———. "A Systematic Management Plan for School Discipline," *NAASP Bulletin,* 61, 405 (January 1977): 1-10.

————. "What Can Students Tell Educators about Classroom Dynamics?" *Theory into Practice,* 16, 3 (June 1977): 262-271.

————. "Who Misbehaves? — A High School Studies Its Discipline Problems," *Educational Administration Quarterly,* 12, 3 (Fall 1976): 65-85.

Duke, Daniel L., and Meckel, Adrienne M. "Disciplinary Rules in American Schools" (Submitted for publication).

Duke, Daniel L. and Perry, Cheryl. "Can Alternative Schools Succeed Where Benjamin Spock, Spiro Agnew, and B. F. Skinner Have Failed?" *Adolescence,* 13, 51 (Fall 1978): 375-392.

Duke, Daniel L., Muzio, Irene A., and Wagner, Lauri. "Gathering Student Perceptions of the Classroom," in *When Teachers and Researchers Cooperate,* edited by Daniel L. Duke (Stanford: Center for Educational Research at Stanford, 1977).

Eash, Maurice J., and Rasher, Sue Pinzur. "Mandated Desegregation and Improved Achievement: A Longitudinal Study," *Phi Delta Kappan,* 58, 5 (January 1977): 394-397.

Ernst, Ken. *Games Students Play* (Millbrae, Calif.: Celestial Arts, 1975).

Etzioni, Amitai. "Organizational Control Structure" in James G. March (ed.), *Handbook of Organizations* (Chicago: Rand McNally & Company, 1965).

Faltico, Gary J. "An After-School School Without Failure: A New Therapy Model for Juvenile Probationers," *Corrective and Social Psychiatry,* 21, 4 (1975): 17-20.

Fisher, Ronald J. "A Discussion Project on High School Adolescents' Perceptions of the Relationship between Students and Teachers," *Adolescence,* 11, 41 (Spring 1976): 87-95).

Gage, N. L., and Berlinger, David. *Educational Psychology* (Chicago: Rand McNally College Publishing Company, 1975).

Gallup, George H. "Eighth Annual Gallup Poll of the Public's Attitudes Toward the Public Schools," *Phi Delta Kappan,* 58, 2 (October 1976): 187-200.

————. "Ninth Annual Gallup Poll of the Public's Attitudes Toward the Public Schools," *Phi Delta Kappan,* 59, 1 (September 1977): 33-48.

Garrison, Karl C., and Cunningham, Ben W. "Personal Problems of Ninth-Grade Pupils," *The School Review,* 60, 1 (January 1952): 30-33.

Gellis, Sydney S., ed. *Yearbook of Pediatrics - 1976* (Chicago: Year Book Medical Publishers, Inc., 1976).

Ginott, Haim G. *Teacher & Child* (New York: Avon Books, 1972).

Glasser, William. *Schools Without Failure* (New York: Harper & Row, Publishers, 1969).

Good, Thomas L., Biddle, Bruce J., and Brophy, Jere E. *Teachers Make a Difference* (New York: Holt, Rinehart and Winston, 1975).

Good, Thomas L., and Brophy, Jere E. *Looking in Classrooms* (New York: Harper & Row, Publishers, 1973).

Gordon, Thomas. *T.E.T.: Teacher Effectiveness Training* (New York: Peter H. Wyden, Publisher, 1974).

Gross, Mel. "Community Involvement Helps Relieve Attendance Problems," *NASSP Bulletin*, 61, 408 (April 1977): 115-116.

Haggerty, Robert J. "The Changing Role of the Pediatrician in Child Health Care," *American Journal of Disturbed Children*, 127 (April 1974): 545-549.

Haines, Gerald L. "The Management Team: Advocates for Kids, a High School Principal's Perspective," *Thrust*, 6, 2 (November 1976): 7-9

Hargreaves, D. H., Hester, S. K., and Mellor, F. J. *Deviance in Classrooms* (London: Routledge & Kegan Paul, 1975), p. 256.

Harvey, Donald L., and Moosha, William G. "In-School Suspension: Does it Work?" *NASSP Bulletin*, 61, 405 (January 1977): 14-17.

Horn, Jack. "Kicked-Out Kids," *Psychology Today*, 9, 7 (December 1975): 83-84.

Hyman, Irwin, *et al.* "Patterns of Interprofessional Conflict Resolution on School Child Study Teams," *Journal of School Psychology*, 11, 3 (Fall 1973): 187-195.

Jacoby, Susan. "What Happened When a High School Tried Self-Government?" *Saturday Review* (April 1, 1972) pp. 49-53.

Janis, Irving L., and Leon Mann. *Decision Making* (New York; The Free Press, 1977).

Johnson, David W. "Students Against the School Establishment: Crisis Intervention in School Conflicts and Organizational Change," *Journal of School Psychology*, 9, 1 (Fall 1971): 84-92.

Kindsvatter, R. "A New View of the Dynamics of Discipline," *Phi Delta Kappan*, 59, 5 (January 1978): 322-325.

Knudten, Richard D. "Delinquency Programs in Schools: A Survey" in Ernst A. Wenk (ed.), *Delinquency Prevention and the Schools*, SAGE Contemporary Social Science Issues 29 (Beverly Hills, Calif.: SAGE Publications, 1976), pp. 53-64.

Kobak, Dorothy. "Teaching Children to Care," *Phi Delta Kappan*, 58, 6 (February 1977): 497.

Kohlberg, Lawrence. "The Cognitive-Developmental Approach to Moral Education," *Phi Delta Kappan,* 56, 10 (June 1975): 670-677.

Kounin, Jacob S. *Discipline and Group Management in Classrooms* (New York: Holt, Rinehart and Winston, Inc., 1970).

Kramer, Jerald. "The East Campus Family Counseling Program,: *Phi Delta Kappan,* 57, 6 (February 1976): 417.

Kvaraceus, William C. "Programs of Early Identification and Prevention of Delinquency" in William W. Wattenberg (ed.), *Social Deviancy among Youth,* The Sixty-Fifth Yearbook of the National Society for the Study of Education, Part 1 (Chicago: The University of Chicago Press, 1966), pp. 189-220.

Lien, Ronald L. "Professional Laboratory Programs in Russia," *The Journal of Teacher Education,* 18, 3 (Fall 1967): 313-319.

Lortie, Dan C. *Schoolteacher* (Chicago: The University of Chicago Press, 1975).

Lucas, William L. "Experiences in a Large City School System" in James M. McPartland and Edward L. McDill (eds.), *Violence in Schools* (Lexington, Mass.: Lexington Books, 1977), pp. 71-76.

Marcus, Lee. "How Teachers View Student Learning Styles," *NASSP Bulletin,* 61, 408 (April 1977): 112-114.

Mackenzie, R. Alec. *The Time Trap: How to Get More Done in Less Time.* (New York: McGraw-Hill Book Company, 1972).

Maslon, Patricia J. "The School Counselor As Collaborative Consultant: A Program for Counseling and Teaching in the Secondary School Classroom," *Adolescence,* 9, 33 (Spring 1974): 97-106.

Maurer, Ada. "Corporal Punishment," *American Psychologist,* 29, 8 (August 1974): 614-626.

McPartland, James M., and McDill, Edward L. "Research on Crime in Schools" in James M. McPartland and Edward L. McDill (eds.), *Violence in Schools* (Lexington, Mass.: Lexington Books, 1977), pp. 3-22.

———. *The Unique Role of Schools in the Causes of Youthful Crime,* Report No. 216 (Baltimore: Center for Social Organization of Schools, 1976).

Metz, M. H. "Clashes in the Classroom: The Importance of Norms for Authority" (A paper presented at the annual meeting of the American Educational Research Association, March 1978).

Morgan, Ronald R. "An Exploratory Study of Three Procedures to Encourage School Attendance," *Psychology in the Schools,* 12, 2 (April 1975): 209-215.

Morissette, Marilyn, and Koshiyama, Albert N. "Student Advocacy in School Discipline: A Look at Suspensions," *Thrust,* 6, 2 (November 1976): 16-18.

Mosher, Ralph L., and Sullivan, Paul R. "A Curriculum in Moral Education for Adolescents," *Journal of Moral Education,* 5, 2 (1976): 159-172.

Mullins, Jerry. "The Interagency Team Concept" in Ruth Pritchard and Virginia Wedra (eds), *A Resource Manual for Reducing Conflict and Violence in California Schools* (Sacramento: California School Boards Association, 1975), pp. 11-16.

NASSP Bulletin. "What Do You Know about Participative Decision Making?" 61, 405 (January 1977).

National Institute of Education. *Violent Schools-Safe Schools* (Washington, D.C.: U.S. Government Printing Office, 1978).

National School Public Relations Association. *Violence and Vandalism* (Arlington, VA: NSPRA, 1975), p. 22.

Nation's Schools. "Crusader for Conciliation?" 89, 6 (June 1972): 33-38.

Neill, George. "Control Specter Hovers as HEW Requests Detailed Reports on Discipline Measures," *Phi Delta Kappan,* 57, 4 (December 1975): 286-287.

Nettler, Gwynn. *Explaining Crime* (New York: McGraw-Hill Book Company, 1974).

Offer, Daniel. "Adolescent Turmoil" in Aaron H. Esman (ed.), *The Psychology of Adolescence* (New York: International Universities Press, Inc., 1975), pp. 141-154.

Peck, Robert F., and Tucker, James A. "Research on Teacher Education" in Robert M. W. Travers (ed.), *Second Handbook of Research on Teaching* (Chicago: Rand McNally & Company, 1973), pp. 940-978.

Powell, Marvin, and Bergem, Jerry. "An Investigation of the Differences between Tenth-, Eleventh-, and Twelfth-Grade 'Conforming' and 'Non-conforming' Boys," *The Journal of Educational Research,* 56, 4 (December 1962): 184-190.

Powell, W. Conrad. "Educational Intervention as a Preventive Measure" in Ernst A. Wenk (ed.), *Delinquency Prevention and the Schools,* SAGE Contemporary Social Science Issues 29 (Beverly Hills, Calif. SAGE Publications, 1976), pp. 105-115.

Raths, Louis E., Harmin, Merrill, and Simon, Sidney B. *Values and Teaching* (Columbus, Ohio: C. E. Merrill Books, 1966).

Robert, Marc. *Loneliness in the Schools* (Niles, Illinois: Argus Communications, 1973).

Rosaler, Jean. *How to Make the Best School Site Council in the World* (Sacramento: California State Department of Education, 1979).

Rosner, Henry Zacharias. "Three Practices to Reach Students," *Personnel and Guidance Journal,* 53, 1 (September 1974): 65-67.

Rubel, Robert. *The Unruly School* (Lexington, Mass.: Lexington Books, 1977).

Rutter, Michael. *Helping Troubled Children* (New York: Plenum Press, 1975).

Ryan, William. *Blaming the Victim* (New York: Pantheon Books, 1971).

St. John, Walter D. "Dealing with Problem Situations," *NASSP Bulletin,* 61, 405 (January 1977): 47-50.

Sanders, Stanley G., and Yarbrough, Janis S. "Bringing Order to an Inner-City Middle School," *Phi Delta Kappan,* 58, 4 (December 1976): 333-334.

Sarason, Seymour. *The Culture of the School and the Problem of Change* (Boston: Allyn and Bacon, Inc., 1971).

Schoenfeld, C. G. "A Psychoanalytic Theory of Juvenile Delinquency," *Crime and Delinquency,* 17, 4 (October 1971): 469-480.

Schrag, Peter. "End of the Impossible Dream," *Saturday Review* (September 19, 1970): 68-69.

Schreck, Robert, *et al.* "The Metamorphosis of Lee High School," *Urban Education,* 10, 2 (July 1975): 198-211.

Sellarole, John and Millins, Jerry. "Management in a Team Structure" in Ruth Pritchard and Virginia Wedra (eds.), *A Resource Manual for Reducing Conflict and Violence in California Schools* (Sacramento: California School Boards Association, 1975), pp. 17-23.

Simon, Herbert. *Administrative Behavior* (New York: The Free Press, 1976).

Sloane, Howard N. Classroom Management (New York: John Wiley and Sons, Inc., 1976).

Smith, Mary Lee, *et al.* Evaluation of the Effects of Outward Bound" in Gene V. Glass (ed.), *Evaluation Studies Review Annual,* vol. 1, 1976 (Beverly Hills, CA: SAGE Publications, 1976), pp. 400-424.

Spady, William G. "The Impact of School Resources on Students" in Fred N. Kerlinger (ed.), *Review of Research in Education,* 1 (Itasca, Illinois: F. E. Peacock Publishers, Inc., 1973), pp. 135-177.

Stebbins, R. A. "The Meaning of Disorderly Behavior: Teacher Definitions of a Classroom Situation," *Sociology of Education*, 44, 2 (Spring 1970): 217-236.

Stenner, A. Jackson, and Mueller, Siegfried G. "A Successful Compensatory Education Model," *Phi Delta Kappan*, 55, 4 (December 1973): 246-248.

Study Commission on Undergraduate Education and the Education of Teachers. *Teacher Education in the United States: The Responsibility Gap* (Lincoln: University of Nebraska Press, 1976).

Surratt, Paul R., Ulrich, Roger, and Hawkins, Robert P. "An Elementary Student as a Behavioral Engineer" in Roger Ulrich, *et al.* (eds.), *Control of Human Behavior* (Glenview, Illinois: Scott, Foresman, 1970), pp. 263-270.

Swift, Marshall, and Back, Linnea. "A Method for Aiding Teachers of the Troubled Adolescent," *Adolescence*, 8, 29 (Spring 1973): 1-16.

Syracuse University Research Corporation. *Disruption in Urban Public Secondary Schools* (Washington, D.C.: National Association of Secondary School Principals, n.d.).

Tannenbaum, Arnold S. "Control in Organizations" in Arnold S. Tannenbaum, ed., *Control in Organizations* (New York: McGraw-Hill Book Company, 1968).

Task Force '74. *The Adolescent, Other Citizens, and Their High Schools* (New York: McGraw-Hill Book Company, 1975).

Thoresen, Carl E. ed. *Behavior Modification in Education*, The Seventy-second Yearbook of the National Society for the Study of Education (Chicago: The University of Chicago Press, 1973).

U.S. Department of Health, Education, and Welfare. *The Education of Adolescents*, The Final Report and Recommendations of the National Panel on High School and Adolescent Education (Washington, D.C.: U.S. Government Printing Office, 1976).

Varenhorst, Barbara B. "Training Adolescents As Peer Counselors," *Personnel and Guidance Journal*, 53, 4 (December 1974): 271-275.

Waller, Willard. *The Sociology of Teaching* (New York: John Wiley & Sons, Inc., 1932).

Wegmann, Robert G. "Classroom Discipline: An Exercise in the Maintenance of Social Reality," *Sociology of Education*, 49, 1 (January 1976): 71-79.

Whimbey, Arthur. *Intelligence Can Be Taught* (New York: E. P. Dutton & Co., Inc. 1975).

Wickman, E. K. *Teachers and Behavior Problems* (New York: The Commonwealth Fund, 1938).

Wynne, Edward. "Adolescent Alienation and Youth Policy," *Teachers College Record,* 78, 1 (September 1976): 23-40.

Zaltman, Gerald and Duncan, Robert. *Strategies for Planned Change* (New York: John Wiley & Sons, Inc., 1977).

Index